Pagan Portals
Dragon Magic

Pagan Portals
Dragon Magic

Rachel Patterson

**MOON
BOOKS**
Winchester, UK
Washington, USA

CollectiveInk

First published by Moon Books, 2024
Moon Books is an imprint of Collective Ink Ltd.,
Unit 11, Shepperton House, 89 Shepperton Road, London, N1 3DF
office@collectiveinkbooks.com
www.collectiveinkbooks.com
www.moon-books.net

For distributor details and how to order please visit the 'Ordering' section on our website.

Text copyright: Rachel Patterson 2023

ISBN: 978 1 80341 444 7
978 1 80341 445 4 (ebook)
Library of Congress Control Number: 2023936008

A CIP catalogue record for this book is available from the British Library.

Design: Lapiz Digital Services

UK: Printed and bound by CPI Group (UK) Ltd, Croydon, CR0 4YY
Printed in North America by CPI GPS partners

We operate a distinctive and ethical publishing philosophy in all areas of our business, from our global network of authors to production and worldwide distribution.

Contents

Disclaimer

Essential oils can be used on the skin for anointing if blended with a base oil, used in an oil burner, for dressing candles or magical tools, added to a ritual bath and used in spells. As a general rule of thumb, I would use ten millilitres of base oil to twenty or twenty-five drops of essential oil. PLEASE test a drop or two on a small area of your skin before you go slapping on loads of oil, just in case you are allergic to it. I also advise blending with a base oil for dressing candles as it will come into contact with your skin. For a blend to use in an oil burner, bath, or diffuser, you can create a blend without using a base oil. Please do source pure essential oils, there are some on the market that have been watered down or have nasty chemicals added.

Never self-medicate, even with herbal remedies. Herbal remedies can be extremely potent; some are toxic. Others can react with prescription or over-the-counter medications in adverse ways. Please do not ingest any herbs if you aren't sure you have identified them correctly. If you are on medication or have health issues, please do not ingest any herbs without first consulting a qualified practitioner.

Here There Be Dragons

He felt the sensation of the dragon rummaging around in his
mind, trying to find a clue to understanding. He half-saw,
half-sensed the flicker of random images, of dragons, of the
mythical age of reptiles and—and here he felt the dragon's
genuine astonishment—of some of the less commendable
areas of human history, which were most of it. And after the
astonishment came the baffled anger. There was practically
nothing the dragon could do to people that they had not,
sooner or later, tried on one another, often with enthusiasm.
You have the effrontery to be squeamish, it thought at him.
But we were dragons. We were supposed to be cruel, cunning,
heartless, and terrible. But this much I can tell you, you ape —
the great face pressed even closer, so that Wonse was staring
into the pitiless depths of his eyes — we never burned and
tortured and ripped one another apart and called it morality.
Terry Pratchett — *Guards! Guards!*

Come with me, let us enter the lair of the dragon...

There are different views of what dragons are and of what they represent. They are sometimes viewed as mythological entities which represent a set of principles. A Dragon viewed as a winged serpent could be a symbol of the earth and the underworld. The wings as a symbol of the heavens. The winged serpent brings together these two principles — as above, so below.

The Chinese dragon is a symbol of Tao, that which is beyond all terms and all polarities but also the force behind all (Yin and Yang). The Dragon represents the unknown, the hidden energy in humans and in nature.

There are various meanings for the word 'dragon'. It stems from Greek, the word 'drakon' which means 'strong one' and 'derkesthai' which translates to 'see clearly' or 'the seeing one'. Some suggestions also suggest it translates as 'the sharp sighted' or 'creature with flashing eyes.[1] Dragon comes from the Latin 'draconem' meaning 'huge serpent, dragon'.

The Greek 'drakon' means 'serpent, giant seafish'. The PIE root word 'derk' meaning 'to see'. Sanskit 'darsata' meaning 'visible'.

In the 13th century, Old French 'dragon' came from the word 'drake' with is Proto Germanic. It is also suggested the origin in Middle English meant 'large serpent' and from Old French, via Latin from Greek 'drakon' meaning 'serpent'.[2]

The Dragon is the principle of clear seeing: the ability to see things in a new light as they really are, beyond all illusions. And I do not believe there can be any doubt about the strength of a dragon from physical, mental to spiritual.

You might be familiar with the idea of a dragon hording his treasure; it is that treasure that symbolises the wisdom it keeps. For us to find the knowledge it guards we must quest for it within ourselves and venture into the unknown to find the answers.

If you have ever practiced yoga, you will know the dragon as the Kundalini, the force that is hidden inside us. We all have it within us to awaken the forces within the dragon.

The World of Dragon has so many different breeds, types, colours, sizes and shapes. Some you may be more familiar with than others — the Chinese or the Welsh Dragon for instance, others such as the Wyrm may be new to you. But no matter what they look like, they all hold incredible power.

A dragon can be a strong, useful and wise guide or guardian and we can also tap into dragon energy to use within our rituals and our magic. Dragons are a primeval force, they are physical and spiritual, they bring with them the full force and power of the elements. They are also very wise and intelligent.

Dragon Energy is one of the most powerful energies I know of and when blended together via the four main elements, creates the etheric dragon... a superpower.

Dragon energy is linear, so be careful what you ask for. You will receive it in the most direct way possible. Be very specific about your intentions, integrity and intelligence. Dragons do not necessarily use human logic, if you offer them a problem they will find a solution, but it will be a straightforward one, removing anything in its path to solve it. Dragon magic often works quickly and can sometimes have unexpected results.

Dragon energy is very good at removing dark energy, it is good for clearing negative energy but make sure you also ask for positive energy to be left in its place.

Before You Start

A dragon should never be engaged in conversation as they are inveterate liars and tricksters, though if you're actually talking to a dragon, you're pretty much toast anyway.
— John Stephens

Whilst I do not want to put you off working with dragons, I would ask you to remember that these are very old and very wise creatures they have a tendency to get bored easily and can be impatient. Always treat them with the respect that you would a wise elder. It will take time and effort to build a relationship with dragons and a lot of practice to understand their magic. You cannot force a dragon to come to you, you cannot make one work for you. If a dragon feels you are worthy and can be trusted, then and only then will they even consider making a first introduction.

Begin by researching and reading as much as you can about dragons, their myths, stories, folklore and legends. Then think about why you want to work with them, what are your reasons and whether you are prepared to put the work and effort in to follow this through properly. Dragon magic is not a quick fix and working with dragons is not something to be taken lightly. I would say only you can decide whether you are ready or prepared to work with dragons but usually they are the ones that make the decision for you.

What I can tell you is that working with dragon energy can be very beneficial and a wonderful experience. Dragons also have so much to teach us, all that ancient wisdom waiting to be shared with us not to mention all their powerful energy and support they can provide us with.

Note: With any kind of magic, you need to put effort, intent and will into it. Just saying a chant or performing the actions of a ritual or spell will not make magic happen. It takes more than just the physical motions. Working with magic of any kind requires commitment and responsibility.

My Dragon Story

Dragons have been a part of my life for as long as I can remember. As a child I was always fascinated with fantasy stories, particularly those that included dragons, witches and wizards. I still have several dragon ornaments from my childhood. Every Saturday morning my dad would take us down to the local library and I would come home with a pile of books to devour. In particular I remember sitting down and reading *Alice's Adventures in Wonderland* from cover to cover in one day. This was closely followed by *Through the Looking Glass* which, of course, has the dragonesque creature, the Jabberwocky. *The Hobbit* was another firm favourite which has since been read and re-read on many occasions, where I met the dragon Smaug. Even earlier I belonged to a book club at school, I remember the excitement each month when the brochure came out and I got to choose a couple of books. One of those was *Green Smoke* by Rosemary Manning, the delightful story of a small dragon living in a cave in Cornwall.

Even before I started my Pagan Witchcraft journey, well over thirty years ago now, dragon magic wove itself into my life. Physically being drawn to dragon ornaments, jewellery and images on clothing but in more subtle ways. My personality has always had a touch of fire dragon to it!

Once I was on my Pagan Witchcraft pathway when my Craft name found me, of course, it contained essence of dragon. The first part being 'Tansy', with my love of native herbals, the second part naturally falling in place as 'Firedragon'.

I cannot remember exactly when my first guardian dragon arrived because it feels as if he has been with me forever. Perhaps I began to acknowledge him once my witchcraft journey began. He is a fire dragon, and he is enormous. When I feel him near, it is a presence looming behind me, literally towering above me, he can appear as several feet taller than me or the size of a house. The size usually depends on how much I have messed up and exactly how irritated he is with my behaviour. His energy is powerful, incredibly so, and he steps in not only to chastise me, but also to offer support, guidance and protection. He has become a part of my energy and I would not want to be without him, even when he gets frustrated with me.

Other dragon energies have come and gone as and when I have needed them whether for spell work, in ritual or just to lend their particular support to whatever I am working on at the time. The interesting thing is that mostly the dragons are fully grown. Rarely do I encounter a young dragon. Although on one particular occasion I was met by a new fresh-faced dragon. We had just finished a sabbat ritual in the centre of Stonehenge and were spending some time connecting with the energy of the stones when a small blue dragon appeared to me. He was very young and new to the world of humans. I had been experiencing a particularly bad time of things personally and I do believe he arrived to help me through it. Not to give advice or support because he was too young for that, but to provide a focus for me to care for him. He travelled with me for some time, until I was back on track.

Once I began to learn about witchcraft, working with dragon magic intensively became second nature. I hope to share some of my passion and experiences with you throughout these pages. I would note that this book is part of the Pagan Portals series, so it provides only an introduction to the world of Dragon Magic. The information here barely scratches the surface of the dragon world. But hopefully it will pique your interest and provide you with a stepping off point to follow your own research. And who knows? Maybe I will write a more comprehensive book on dragons one day too!

Your journey will be your own, and may well be very different from mine, but what it will be is a definite adventure.

Part I

Dragon Beginnings

The Origin Story

Did not learned men, too, hold, till within the last twenty-five years, that a flying dragon was an impossible monster? And do we not now know that there are hundreds of them found fossil up and down the world? People call them Pterodactyles: but that is only because they are ashamed to call them flying dragons, after denying so long that flying dragons could exist.

— Charles Kingsley

Where did dragons originate from? It is a good question and one that I do not believe has a definitive answer, however, I do have some suggestions. Dragons appear in mythology across the globe, nearly every country has dragon stories. Such a widespread myth, must have some kind of creation or back story, surely?

One of the main theories is derived from the discovery of dinosaur bones. Particularly during the 1600s when historians began to make such discoveries. One of the most notable was from English man, Robert Plot, who found a huge bone that he believed to be the thigh bone of a giant.[3]

There happily came to Oxford while I was writing of this, a living Elephant to be shown publicly at the ACT, An. 1676, with whose Bones ... I compared ours; and found those of the Elephant not only of a different Shape, but also incomparably different to ours, though the Beast were very young and not half grown. If then they are neither the Bones of Horses, Oxen, nor Elephants, as I am strongly persuaded they are not ... It remains, that (notwithstanding their extravagant Magnitude) they must have been the bones of Men or Women: Nor doth any thing hinder but they may have been so, provided it be clearly made out, that there have been Men and Women of proportionable Stature in all Ages of the World, down even to our own Days (Plot, 1677).

The bone turned out to be a leg bone from the Megalosaurus bucklandi, a predator from the Jurassic and early Cretaceous period.

In Austria 1335 a huge skull was found in a gravel pit near Klagenfurt. It was believed to be the skull from an old legend of a water dragon that brought floods to the town. The skull was displayed in the town hall for many years and is now in a museum there. In 1590 they created a Lindwurm statue for the capital Carinthia, based on the skull, it represents a dragon that spouts water. During the 1800s the skull was identified as that of an Ice Age woolly rhinoceros.[4]

Another famous dragon skeleton was the work of Dr Albert Koch.[5] He exhibited a sea dragon skeleton in New York, 1845. The 35m (114') creature consisted of a large skull complete with teeth and a long snake like body. He called the creature a 'Hydrarchos', suggesting it was a 'blood thirsty monarch of the waters'. Until he was called out by a professor, Jeffries Wyman, who spotted the skeleton was made up from several different species of animal, mostly whales. History is littered with stories such as these, all of which were either cases of mistaken identity or hoaxes.

Going back even further in time to the first century CE and to the site of the Himalayas where we find a traveller, Apollonius of Tyana[6]. He notes that the whole area was 'full of dragons'. He claimed to have seen many dragon skulls. Roll forward in time and it is believed he had found fossils from a crocodile type dinosaur mixed in with those of an extinct elephant. Around 484 BCE a Greek philosopher called Herodotus wrote about seeing bones from 'winged serpents' whilst in Arabia. It is assumed that what he saw were the fossilised bones of Pterosaurs.[7] Again, these types of stories are found across history and the globe.

Many ancient myths and ancient stories contain tales of dragon like beasts. In the Hindu Vedas we find the Vrtra, a 'shoulderless' being, a snake like creature.

I will tell the heroic deeds of Indra, those which the Wielder of the Thunderbolt first accomplished. He slew the dragon and released the waters; he split open the bellies of the mountain. He slew the dragon who lay upon the mountain; Tvastr fashioned the roaring thunderbolt for him. Like lowing cows, the waters have flowed straight down to the ocean...Indra, when you killed the first born of dragons and over came the deluding lures of wily, at that very moment you brough forth the sun, heaven and dawn.[8]

The cosmic goddess, Tiamat from the Babylonian Epic of Creation[9] is said to have created a whole host of monsters to attack the gods. It is also suggested that she herself is in the form of a monstrous serpent.

In Egyptian mythology a serpent, Apophis/Apep[10] attacks the boat of the sun god Ra and is slashed into pieces, only to rise again the next night. Presumably the beast is the night or dark in opposition to Ra and his light.

The Psalms include mention of dragons too, as in Psalm 74:

You divided the sea by Your strength; You broke the heads of the sea serpents in the waters.

Interestingly, depending on the version of Bible you look at the word 'serpents' is sometimes replaced with 'monster' or 'dragon'. In fact, dragons are mentioned several times in the Bible. Mostly it seems in reference to Satan or the Devil.

The great dragon was hurled down — that ancient serpent called the devil, or Satan, who leads the whole world astray. He was hurled to the earth, and his angels with him.[11]

Of course, no self-respecting Greek myth would be without mention of a dragon or 'drakon' which covers all kinds of serpents, snakes and dragon type creatures. We find serpent like Dracones, watery Cetea, fire breathing Chimaera and the Dracaenae.[12]

During the 3rd and 4th Centuries Roman and Byzantine cavalry units carried a 'draco', a military standard. This standard was a dragon shaped wind sock type affair made from fabric with a metal head designed to catch the wind and move like a serpent.[13]

Germanic and Scandinavian tales do not escape from the clutches of dragon mania either. Scandinavian mythology includes the[14] World Serpent for instance.[15] Chieftains and kings rode in large longships or 'dragonships' that bore carved dragon heads on the bow.

His dragon with her sails of blue, all bright and brilliant to the view[16]

Another suggestion is that people have mistaken giant reptiles for dragons. Somewhere along the line humans developed a fear and even hatred of reptiles, we also have a tendency to exaggerate. Are some of the dragon stories formed from someone seeing a particularly large crocodile and embellishing their story? There are a plethora of stories relating to the sighting of giant reptile, huge crocodiles, giant lizards and the like.

A most fascinating job title of cryptozoologist exists, it is someone who studies mysterious animals, those believed to be extinct (or not) and those creatures unknown to modern science. Dragons fall under this category. Cryptozoology turns up a myriad of sightings and experiences with creatures that would be classified as dragons. I am not just talking about folk stories and tales of old, but modern-day happenings across the globe from giant serpents and sea creatures to flying winged dragons.

There is also the fear of the unknown and I believe this comes into play when looking at the depths of the oceans. Those deep dark areas of the sea that are so vast and far down they have never been investigated. We naturally fear deep water, it is part of our DNA to do so. Is this perhaps another home for water dragons, hidden from the prying eyes of humans? There is certainly a good amount of information that supports dragons love of water.

In some cases, the dragon is used a symbol for darkness in the form of plague, storms or floods. Dragons also appear in several creation stories, relating them to the cosmos. Once Christianity took hold the dragon does appear to have been used as a symbol for evil works or the devil in some form.

I could continue on and in more depth with the history of dragons in mythology and folklore, it is a huge subject. But as this book is just an introduction and primarily focused on dragon magic, I shall have to dig myself out from this particular rabbit hole, for now. Or perhaps that should be from a knucker hole?

The question as to the origin of dragons has not been answered here, and I doubt you will find it anywhere to be honest. Is the source derived from finding dinosaur bones? Possibly. Or perhaps it is the dragon being used as a collective description for man's own fears. We still carry a 'flight or fight' response in our subconscious to this day and perhaps that is at least in part a reason for creating the idea of a dragon beast.

Or maybe, just maybe, and this is my belief, dragons are and always have been...real.

What Is a Dragon?

The ultimate challenge of a teacher lies not in the slaying
of dragons, but rather in exposing them as beasts no longer
to be feared. — Alan Burton

If you were to picture a dragon in your mind right now, what would it look like? Chances are it would have a large scaly body, long tail with ridges, a pair of wings, four legs and a scaly horse shaped head (this image is known as the Heraldic dragon). Throw in fire breathing and you would have probably the most popular image. But there are so many different types and designs of creature that fall under the dragon category from snakelike limbless beasts to ornate colourful Chinese dragons and every possible design in between. Poisonous and/or fiery breath features quite often and the ability to coil itself around features in the landscape. Wings also appear, but not on every type of dragon. Some stories describe creatures with no legs, the dragon being more of a snakelike serpent. Others tell of beasts with two legs or four. Claws or talons are often spoken of, particularly in the case of unsuspecting humans or livestock being grabbed by them. Size seems to vary, although most legends just describe the dragon being 'huge' or 'enormous', giving no particular measurements.

Dragon Habitat

It does not do to leave a live dragon out of your calculations,
if you live near him. — J. R. R. Tolkien

Where will you find a dragon, what is its natural habitat? Probably for most people your first thoughts will go to a cave and that is a good starting point. Many stories tell of dragons living in caves or under mountains, often sitting on their hoard of gold. Folklore tells of buried treasures, usually under a mountain so it stands to reason a dragon would guard it to keep people from digging it up. Sea monsters and serpents obviously live in the dark depths under the water. However, you are just as likely to find a dragon living in the middle of a forest, a valley or in mountain ranges. In fact, certain types of English dragon, the Knucker, live at the bottom of deep dark water filled holes in the ground. Do not be limited by the idea of caves. It does seem that water of some kind is often a feature in the landscape where a dragon decides to take up residence. If you fancy doing some research in your local area, a good starting point is place names. Anywhere that includes the word Dragon, Drake or Worm (or the equivalent in the native language) could mean the presence of a dragon legend.

Hoards

Sleeping on a dragon's hoard with greedy, dragonish thoughts in his heart, he had become a dragon himself. — C.S. Lewis

Some stories tell of dragons sitting on a hoard of treasure, gold and precious jewels. Often these are hidden away at the base of mountains or burial mounds. Britain in particular has a number of barrows bearing names that refer to dragons. Barrow is the name given to ancient burial mounds in England, large structures shaped from piles of soil over a place where people were buried. A lot of these names are still in use but the stories and legends attached to them have been lost over time. In Garsington, Oxfordshire a barrow has been known as 'Dragon Hoard' since the 13th century. Wolverley in Worcestershire has a site named 'Drakelowe'. Over in Devon it is said a dragon flies from the hill fort on Dolbury Hill over to Cadbury Castle every night, or back the other way, lighting up the sky with his flaming breath as he guards treasures held beneath both places. A local rhyme says:

> *If Cadbury Castle and Dolbury Hill delven were*
> *All England might plough with a golden share*[17]

Over in Wales dragon tales abound, only these dragons guard their treasure in wooded areas and on small hills. These dragons guard their treasure diligently, there doesn't seem to be a folk tale attached to the locations telling of dragons terrorising nearby villages or feeding on livestock. It seems most of these dragons are so dedicated to their hoard that they stay there on guard, for eternity.

Fair Maidens

A general theme with dragon tales seems to be the offering and devouring of young maidens. Often this is along the lines of the villages demanding the dragon stops eating all their livestock and instead they offer up a regular supply of young ladies from the village. This has always befuddled me. What would you rather give to a hungry dragon, a regular supply of sheep or your daughters? Doesn't make any sense to me!

An example is found in the story of the Stoorworm from Scotland[18]. A terrible sea monster arrived, levelling towns and eating everyone in sight, his breath poisoning all living things. The king sought help from a local wizard who advised the beast must be fed seven maidens at dawn every week. The beast was happy with the exchange and his rampages were kept at bay. Obviously, the people grew tired of offering up seven maidens each week and the story has a happy ending with the hero killing the dragon and marrying a princess, not such a happy ending for the Stoorworm, of course.

Feeding Dragons

*Noontime was absolutely the perfect time for a duel in the
dragon's opinion as this was also lunchtime, his favorite part
of the day. As the saying went, he could kill two birds with
one stone.* — Sully Tarnish

Fair maidens aside, because it seems terribly wasteful and
would take a lot of effort to keep up the supply, it appears
dragons are very fond of milk. The idea perhaps stems from
the belief that snakes love a drop of milk, many cultures have
beliefs that a dish of milk should be left out to appease the local
snake population. It follows then, that a lot of dragon tales
include offerings of milk, although the saucer would need to be
much larger. The legend of The Lambton Worm from Durham
in England states the beast would sit wrapped around a local
hill (called Worm Hill) nine times and became:

*...the terror of the county, and amongst other enormities levied
a daily contribution of nine cows' milk, which was always placed
for it at the green hill and in default of which it devoured man
and beast.*[19]

Of course, a lot of stories tell of dragons eating sheep and other
livestock in addition to fair maidens so they are definitely
omnivores.

Dragon Offspring

Interestingly most dragon legends and tales describe fully
grown dragons who just appear from nowhere as adults. Very
few stories go into details of where the dragon originated from
or tell of baby sized dragons. There are a few baby dragon
legends, of course, although they seem rare. The Mordiford

Dragon[20] from Herefordshire in England, was found as a baby by a little girl who took it home. Her parents were horrified and instructed her to get rid of the 'wicked creature'. She didn't, of course, and hid the baby dragon, feeding it on milk. It grew and once fully grown decided livestock was tastier than milk and then as you would expect, it progressed to eating humans.

There are beliefs in some cultures that dragons are born from piles of dead bodies on battlefields, seemingly combusting into existence from the remains. Other beliefs include a woman allowing a snake to suckle at her breast which would change the creature into a monstrous flying snake complete with scales and wings.

Dragon Slayers

The townspeople took the prince for dead
When he never returned with the dragon's head
When with her, he stayed
She thought he'd be too afraid
But he loved her too much instead.
— Jess C. Scott

Much as a it pains me to write about them, I do feel the need to briefly mention the role of dragon slayers as they do feature in a large amount of the legends. Personally, I usually root for the dragon in these scenarios, but history it seems favours the slayer. Often these heroes are knights clad in shining armour wielding large swords. This image may stem from the Arthurian legends and tales of one of the most famous dragon slayers, St George. Saints do seem to be favourites for the role of dragon slayer, perhaps there is a link here to Christianity and the idea of the saint banishing the dragon or slaying it being a metaphor? The dragon in the scenario being perhaps unbelievers of the

Christian faith or Pagans. Just to bring about some balance, there are legends where the hero successfully kills the dragon, only then to succumb to death himself either from his wounds inflicted during the battle or being taken out by the dragon with its dying breath (literally). In Somerset, England, a dragon living in a hillside cave caused havoc. One story claims the hero, John of Aller[21] was a peasant, others say he was a knight. He battled with the dragon eventually killing it with his spear. The dragon kills John with his dying breath, burning him with the flames.

Dragon Lines

Below the earth's surface, deep within her body, there is a web of energy that courses beneath that which we can see. If you were to visualise this energy it would look like a lattice work of veins and where these energy lines cross each other it creates a concentration of energy that have come to be regarded as sacred places that hold great power. At these points you will often find standing stones, burial mounds, wells and springs, earthworks, castles or churches. Many cultures have known about these hidden lines of energy often called ley lines, they are Fairy paths to the Irish, Dragon lines by the Chinese, Spirit Lines to the Peruvians and Dream Paths to the Aborigines. You can check online to see if there are any dragon lines in your area. I recommend standing on the line, bare feet, if possible, particularly if there is a point where the lines intersect. Tap into that energy and feel the power of dragons.

Year of the Dragon

The Chinese zodiac features twelve animals, each year featuring one of those animals in a twelve-year cycle. The fifth animal in the Chinese zodiac is the dragon. 2024 is a year of the Dragon and they repeat every twelve years after that. The Chinese year runs from early to mid-February around to the end of January.

The type of dragon alternates each time between gold, water, wood, fire and earth. 2024 brings the reign of the Wood Dragon. The Dragon symbolises power, nobility, honour, luck and success.

Dragons in the Stars

One of the largest constellations in our skies in the northern celestial hemisphere is Draco.[22] The constellation represents the dragon that guarded the gardens of Hesperides in Greek mythology. The Greek astronomer, Ptolemy was the first to record this constellation in the 2nd century. Draco is a circumpolar constellation and never sets below the horizon in the northern hemisphere. The position of the stars within this constellation, when joined together by a line map out the shape of a dragon.

Dragon Colours

Images of dragons created by artists throughout history tend to focus on dragons being a shade of green, red or sometimes brown/bronze. Perhaps keeping the focus on the suggested colour of dinosaurs or the lizards that we have now? In my experience my own dragon guardian is red, but I have worked with dragons in various colours. I find the dragon will often take on the colour to represent the element that they channel, so an earth dragon would be green or brown, an air dragon would be yellow or white, a fire dragon is red and a water dragon blue. I have also found the chaos dragon to be a dark shade of purple. Sometimes the colour also represents the habitat they live in, so a dragon from a desert area might be yellow and a dragon from snowy icy climbs would be white or silver. I have a sneaky suspicion that some of them can actually change their colours to suit their moods. I do not hold with the idea that dark colours make bad dragons and light colours make good ones, it doesn't seem to work that way.

Part II

Myths, Legends and Stories

Dragons in Fiction

Possibly the first experience we have with dragons is within the pages of a book. As children there are plenty of dragons in fictional story books, cartoons or TV shows. Some of them are portrayed in better ways than others, but we learn from all of them. Here are just a few of my favourites.

Smaug

> *My armour is like tenfold shields, my teeth are swords, my claws spears, the shock of my tail is a thunderbolt, my wings a hurricane, and my breath death!*[23]

One of the most well-known dragons in fictional work, he appears in J. R. R. Tolkien's book, *The Hobbit*. He is a fire drake who lives in the Lonely Mountain guarding treasure amassed by the Dwarves. He hibernated within the mountain for 171 years until a company of Dwarves awoke him. Smaug was unimpressed and retaliated by wreaking havoc upon the nearby Lake-town until he was slain by Bard the Bowman. Said to be male and golden in colour with red eyes. His size appears to be unknown and suggestions have been made anywhere between 18 and 130 metres. Suffice to say I believe he was quite large.

Jabberwocky

> *Beware the Jabberwock, my son!*
> *The jaws that bite, the claws that catch!*[24]

A huge dragon like creature from C S Lewis' book, *Through the Looking Glass*. He appears in a poem within the book that Alice reads. In an illustration by Tenniel, he is depicted as a large winged chimera with the body of a dragon, a fish like head, antennae and taloned hands on its wings and arms.

Harry Potter

What's life without a few dragons?[25]

The Harry Potter series of books by author J. K. Rowling feature several different types of dragons, notably in the Triwizard Tournament. The Hungarian Horntail was the breed Harry had to face in the tournament. With huge wings, horns and spikes and, of course fire, breathing it was quite formidable. The Norwegian Ridgeback was the egg Hagrid reared; he named the baby dragon Norbert. This type of dragon appears to be quite toxic. The Romanian Longhorn has, as the name suggests, long horns that it uses to gore its prey. Dragon heart strings were also used in the making of wands for the wizards and their blood and powdered horn is used in potions. One of the main characters, Draco Malfoy's name derives from the Latin Dragon constellation, Draco.

The Last Dragon Chronicles Collection

Everyone wants to believe in something that will make their mundane lives more bearable and their inevitable death less … final.[26]

This collection of stories by Chris d'Lacey ranks among my favourite dragon tales. The books are equally charming, funny and deep. It starts with a collection of clay dragons that come to life and follows the story of David on his quest to uncover the mysteries and the legends that surround dragons. Truly enchanting series, I love them and the depiction of dragons within the pages.

Discworld

This is where the dragons went.

They lie...

Not dead, not asleep. Not waiting, because waiting implies expectation. Possibly the word we're looking for here is...

...dormant.

And although the space they occupy is not like normal space, nevertheless they are packed in tightly. Not a cubic inch there is but is filled by a claw, a talon, a scale, the tip of a tail, so the effect is like one of those trick drawings and your eyeballs eventually realize that the space between each dragon is, in fact, another dragon.

They could put you in mind of a can of sardines, if you thought sardines were huge and scaly and proud and arrogant.

And presumably, somewhere, there's the key.[27]

I could not leave out the dragons that appear in the *Discworld* series by my favourite author Sir Terry Pratchett, yes, I am a confirmed 'Kevin'. Discworld dragons can fly, breathe fire, and tend to explode due to their unstable digestive systems. On the Discworld there are four species of dragon: draco nobilis, draco vulgaris, draco lunaris and draco stellar nauticae. *Guards! Guards!* Features a female Noble dragon that is summoned and used to terrify the inhabitants of Ankh-Morpork. Smaller dragons are featured in several of the Discworld novels, kept in the safety of Lady Ramkin's Dragon Sanctuary, known as the Sunshine Sanctuary for Sick Dragons. These smaller dragons are of the swamp variety and often kept as pets. Sam Vimes has one called Errol (real name Goodboy Bindle Featherstone of Quirm). Pratchett understands dragons, as he does with most subjects including humans and magic.

Dragons from Mythology

People who deny the existence of dragons are often eaten by dragons. From within. — Ursula K. Le Guin

Myths and legends have a huge amount of dragon information that we can use to work with. Here I have included a random selection and my recommendations for the magic that can be worked with them. If you find one that appeals, I would recommend reading the myths and stories written about them before approaching them.

Jörmungandr

The World serpent or mighty snake from Norse legends is Jörmungandr. The Norse beliefs include the cosmos having three levels which are home to nine worlds which house the gods, dwarfs, elves, giants and humans. At the top the level is Asgard, the home of the gods and Valhalla, where Odin sits with those souls that have fallen in battle. In the middle is Midgard or middle earth, this is where we the humans reside along with the giants. In the bottom level you find Hel, a frozen world where souls of those who have passed from old age can be found alongside those that are being punished in the afterlife. Midgard is surrounded by a large ocean and that is where you find Jörmungandr coiling itself around the circumference completing a circle by biting its own tail.

Jörmungandr magical characteristics: Infinity and pretty much anything you need, Jörmungandr covers all kinds of magic

Lambton Worm

Perhaps one of the most well-known British dragon legends belongs to that of the Lambton Worm[28]. Lambton is set in the county of Durham in north east England and our story takes place in the area of the Lambton estate. The legend can be found in folk tales and many old story books from the area. Our story begins with Sir John Lambton, heir to the Lambton estate although by all accounts, not a particularly enthusiastic or reliable type of chap. As was his custom on a Sunday he would go fishing, on this particular occasion he became frustrated at the lack of fish activity at which point he *'vented his disappointment at his ill success in curses loud and deep'*. Some while later he felt his line begin to tug and after some great physical effort, he pulled his catch to land. To his horror it was not a fish but instead he had caught an unsightly worm. He removed it from the hook and threw it with disgust into a nearby well. Casting his line again he settled down until a passer-by asked him *'what sport?'* to which he replied that he believed he had *'catched the Devil'* and pointed to the well. The worm was left in the well but grew each day in both size and strength. Until it became so large it couldn't fit in the well and had to seek new accommodation. During the day it took to laying coiled around a rock in the river and at night it set itself around the base of a neighbouring hill. Eventually it was so large that it could coil its body around the base of the hill three times. By now it was terrorising the land, eating the livestock and drinking any available milk. Once it had exhausted all supplies on one side of the hill it ventured across the river towards Lambton Hall. He was met by the old Lord, the young heir having gone off to war. The old Lord instructed his staff to prepare a large trough in the courtyard and fill it with milk. This became a routine with the dragon returning each morning for its trough full of milk. If the milk was there, it would cause no damage or harm, if it was empty or only half full the beast would cause great damage to the surrounding land. Many knights and brave men attempted to slay the dragon to no avail. They would often cut limbs from the beast, which just regrew.

Seven years later the young heir returned and on hearing the tale of the dragon he ventured out to meet it, but first visited a Sybil (soothsayer/prophetess). He was told the situation was all of his own doing and that he must don his chain mail and make a stand on the rock in the middle of the river. Part of the advice also stated he must make a solemn vow to protect all of nature and after killing the dragon he must slay the first living thing he met, failure to do so would cause the next nine generations of Lambtons to die in terrible circumstances. The beast and the knight met at the rock where the knight struck the dragon with his sword, which didn't seem to have any affect other than to annoy the dragon (not a big surprise). The dragon wrapped its coils around the knight in an attempt to strangle him. Unfortunately for the dragon, the knight's armour had large spikes on which inflicted many wounds, the more the dragon squeezed. The dragon uncoiled and as it did so the knight struck, cutting the dragon in two. One half of the dragon was carried away on the current of the river, meaning it could not be reunited and the dragon was finally defeated.

The young Lambton returned to the house and was met by his father, remembering the prediction, he did not want to kill his father, being the first living thing he met, so he called his hound and killed it instead. Sadly, this did not fulfil the promise and the prediction of the nine-generation curse was set.

Lambton magical characteristics: Self-confidence, growth, transitions, transformation, nature magic, protection, truth, promises/vows, curses

Quetzalcoatl

The Quetzalcoatl is a Mayan feathered snake dragon seen as a god. He created the fifth cycle of mankind by using ancestral ashes and bones. Quetzalcoatl was a benevolent god who brought culture to humans in the form of reading and books. He could shape shift into a human either as an old man with a white beard or a young man with feathers in his hair.

Quetzalcoatl magical characteristics: Creativity, ancestors, culture, the arts, shape shifting

Vritra

The Hindu hymns of the Rig Veda tell the tale of the god Indra and the serpent dragon Vritra.[29] In this case the dragon, Vritra, represents drought and the warrior Indra sets out to remove this threat. Indra begins by drinking a plant based ritual potion called Soma. On facing the dragon Vritra, Indra attacks with his weapon that unleashes a lightning bolt. Vritra obviously responds and lashes at Indra with his coiled tail, hitting him in the face. Indra continues onwards, lifting Vritra up high and throwing him to the ground which kills him. Not content with killing just one dragon, Indra also kills Vritra's mother, Danu. It is this battle that ensures the waters return to the land and the drought is ended. Later on, in the Purana the story of Indra and Vritra changes to show Vritra swallowing Indra, then being made by the other gods to vomit him up. The god Vishnu instructs that Indra must not attack Vritra again with any weapons or with anything wet or dry and not during the day or the night. Indra is patient and eventually spies Vritra at twilight, which makes it not day or night, but in between. Indra shape shifts into foam on the ocean waves, making him neither wet nor dry and he attacks and kills Vritra by strangling the creature. Vritra's body explodes and releases water to parch the dry lands and it begins to rain. The dragon Vritra is described as being a Nāga.

Vritra magical characteristics: Defence, water magic

Nāga Dragon Kings

Mucalinda is a nāga King. In Buddhism the nāga is seen as a beast that can teach us lessons, how to understand and unravel the mysteries of life, thus allowing us to reach enlightenment. In one myth from the Mahavagga, Buddha was meditating under a Bodhi tree when a storm picked up.[30] The King Mucalinda saw that Buddha was deep in meditation and was in impending danger from the storm. Mucalinda coiled himself around Buddha seven times and raised his hooded head above him. The storm lasted for seven days, when it was finished Mucalinda uncoiled from Buddha, leaving him safe. Just to bring about balance, there is a further story where Buddha is visiting a monastery and asks to stay the night in the sacred firehouse. He is warned that a fierce Dragon King resides there, but Buddha decides to stay anyway. Buddha makes himself comfortable in the firehouse and sits cross legged on the floor where he is met by the Dragon King who spits out a cloud of smoke towards him. In retaliation Buddha returns fire with his own cloud of smoke. The Dragon King responds by sending a blast of fire towards Buddha, which is met and returned by Buddha with a stronger fire. By this point the whole firehouse is seemingly ablaze. The Dragon King is humbled and defeated, at which point Buddha picks up the dragon and drops him into his dish. Buddha tells his hosts *"his power was overcome by my power"*.

It seems Buddha meets nāgas on quite a regular basis, each encounter showing the power of the dragon but also those of Buddha. Each myth shows the power of nature but also the balance of good and evil.

Nāga Dragon Kings magical characteristics: Knowledge, mysteries, enlightenment, understanding, protection, humility, balance

The Chinese Long Dragon

Picture a world that is flooded. The Yellow Emperor, Huangdi, is fighting against a rebellion led by the god of war, Chiyou. Huangdi calls upon Yinglong,[31] the 'responding dragon' to attack Chiyou. Yinglong begins by collecting all the flood waters into his stomach with the idea he might release them and drown Chiyou. In his defence, Chiyou calls on Feng Bo, the wind god and Yu Shi, the rain god for help. Huangdi responds by asking the goddess, Ba, to create a drought. This allows the dragon, Yinglong, to attack whereupon he kills Chiyou. This is one of the stories told of Yinglong that appear in the Shanhaijing. Yinglong is seen as a dragon of nature with power of the seas, land and weather. Yinglong often appears in images with a traditional dragon shape with four legs and a long snake like tail with a horse shaped head. He is often depicted with whiskers and a pearl under his throat, which symbolises wisdom, power and prosperity. Numbers feature prominently in the Chinese Long Dragon too, with the number of scales totalling 117, 81 of those being positive and 36 being negative. Yinglong represents life force, the positive masculine energy and the negative feminine vibes. The Yin and Yang.

Chinese Long Dragon magical characteristics: Nature, weather magic, water magic, wisdom, power, prosperity, balance

Japanese Ryūjin Dragon

Deep beneath the sea in a red and white palace made of coral you will find the Dragon god, Ryūjin,[32] master of the waters and God of the sea. This beastie can command the tides and swallow whole ships. He is generally quiet and amenable, unless you disrespect him, or the oceans and his retaliation is disastrous. This dragon can also shape shift into human form which allows him to take human partners. Ryūjin is said to be the grandfather of the first Japanese emperor.

Ryūjin magical characteristics: Water magic, power, shape shifting, ancestors

Ti'amat

From ancient Babylonia we find a myth telling the story of an epic cosmic battle between order and chaos.[33] Marduk is our hero representing the divine world who is set against Ti'amat, the goddess of disorder and death who also happens to be a dragon. Of course, I am rooting for the dragon, but as with most of these stories it doesn't end well. There is a lot of detail to this story, if it interests you, do seek out the whole myth. Here I have included a short summary.

Marduk was the champion of the gods and rode a storm chariot pulled by a team of horses. Dressed in armour, his tools were a mace, a bow and a quiver and he could throw lightening. His words formed into an enchantment and he held herbs to protect against poison. As he drew near to Ti'amat her forces surrounded him. Ti'amat cast a spell to win him over to her side, but his enchantment deflected hers. He challenged Ti'amat to meet him one on one. He called upon the winds and storms to trap her. So, they met in the middle to fight. Ti'amat opened her jaws with the intention of swallowing Marduk, but the storms he had conjured up entered her mouth instead and filled her stomach with their power, keeping her jaws forced open. This allowed Marduk to shoot an arrow straight into her mouth and down through her heart. Ti'amat was dead. Not content with just killing her, Marduk trampled over her torso, shattered her skull and tore open her body. Half of this he used to create the sky and the other half he used to form the earth. As he opened her ribs, he made a gate for the sun. Her spit became the rain clouds and her breasts and tail created the landscape. Ti'amat's eye sockets became two rivers and Marduk laid out her intestines across the ruins of Apsu where he created a place of worship for the gods when they descended to earth. Here the temple of Esharra was built. Marduk threw Ti'amat's offspring into the sky to create the eleven constellations.

Ti'amat magical characteristics: Chaos, magic, nature, divine connection

Zilant or Ajdaha

A dragon from Russian and Turkic legends who represents the city of Kazan. The Zilant seems to be the Russian name but referred to in Persian history as Ajdaha or Ajdaha-yilan (dragon-snake) The Zilant is a cross between a Western and Wyvern with two wings and two limbs. It has the body of a bird, a dragon head, chicken limbs, sharp teeth, red wings, scaly dark skin and dark feathers. Some stories tell of this dragon being a benevolent one, helping humans and often giving out gifts and wealth. In other parts it wasn't so positive in its behaviour.[34] One tale tells of a beautiful woman who went to fetch water from the Qazansu river, she made a complaint to the boss of the city that it was not situated in a convenient place. Her advice to him was to move the city. Bizarrely, the boss man agreed. However, the spot the lady had chosen was infested with huge snakes, the leader of which was a two headed beast, Zilant. One of his heads ate grass, the other feasted on young virgins. The boss man (called a Khan) sought advice from a wizard who instructed him to build a wood and straw hut near the hill. In the spring the snakes emerged from their winter hibernation and headed for the straw. Once the snakes had found the straw a local knight was despatched to set fire to the straw, killing all the snakes. The smell from the burning snakes was quite deadly and poisoned many people and animals close by. However, the two headed dragon, Zilant managed to escape heading to the Qaban lakes. It is here that he still resides, and on occasion takes his revenge on the locals.

Zilant magical characteristics: Revenge, wealth

Apollo and Python

In the ancient Greek myths, you will find various versions of the Apollo and Python story.[35] The god, Apollo, travels to Delphi in some stories where he is digging foundations for a shrine and discovers a female dragon who has been terrorising the locals, so he kills her. In other stories he goes to Delphi and is barred from entering a shrine by a dragon, who he fights and kills. They follow the same theme with Apollo defeating the dragon, usually with an arrow, sometimes hundreds of arrows. Python is an enormous dragon serpent who guards the sacred Oracle of Delphi. One story tells that Python was born of the rotting slime that was left behind after the Great Deluge. Python was also said to be the child of Gaea (Earth).

Python magical characteristics: Divination, earth magic

The Hydra and Herakles

Herakles[36] (Hercules in the Roman pantheon) was the child of a god and a human who earnt a place in the Greek Olympian pantheon. All his stories of heroism include a mythical beast, three of them are dragons. One of these myths involves a serpent with many heads, a Hydra. The dragon was terrorising the lands killing people and livestock. The Hydra began with nine heads, one of them immortal. Each time one of the immortal heads was severed, two more grew in its place. When Herakles took on the hydra in battle, its heads numbered over a hundred. Herakles rode in a chariot to meet the dragon in battle bringing with him, Iolaos. They carried flaming brands with them; each time Herakles chopped off one of the Hydra's heads, Iolaos used the fiery brand to cauterise the stump, this stopped another head from growing. Systematically Herakles chopped off each head and Iolaos cauterised the stump until only the one immortal head remained. This last head was removed by Herakles sword and the dragon lay down dead, lying in a pool of its own poisonous blood.

Hydra magical characteristics: Death and rebirth, renewal

St Michael and the Dragon

Found in the Book of Revelation by St John, the book states:

> *...was no longer any place for them in heaven. And the Great Dragon was cast out, that ancient serpent, who is called the Devil and Satan, the deceiver of the whole world. He was thrown down to the earth and his angels were thrown down with him.*[37]

This shows the dragon as a representation of all that is evil, equated to the Devil who was battled by good in the form of St Michael. Further on in the book it continues with the dragon being on earth and causing havoc.[38]

Further on and the dragon is described as having ten heads who is then buried for a thousand years. Once the thousand years are over, he will be let loose but fire will come down from the heavens and the dragon is thrown into the lake of fire and sulphur.[39]

Another example of good in the form of angels and evil being portrayed as a dragon.

St Michael's Dragon magical characteristics: Chaos, darkness

St George and the Dragon

I guess no dragon book would be complete without the tale of St George and the Dragon, possibly one of the most famous dragon slayers.[40] St George of Cappadocia (Turkey) was adopted by English knights on their crusades as their patron saint following their visit to a church in Lydda (Lod, Israel) which was sacred to the memory of St George. Early stories of St George and his quests do not include a dragon, this seems to have emerged much later. The story begins in a large city which had a lake that was home to a dragon. The usual story follows with the dragon terrifying the land and the people that lived there. It ate the livestock and killed people with its poisonous breath. Once they had run out of sheep the King decreed that his people offer up their children on a system of drawing lots. Eventually the city was running low on viable offspring and the lot fell on to the King's daughter. After much argument from the King, the maiden was offered up to the dragon. Whilst she sat awaiting her fate a knight appeared on his horse (well, that was lucky, wasn't it?). This was, of course, George, who galloped on his horse towards the dragon with his lance in hand. Thrusting the lance straight into the open mouth of the dragon he managed to pin it to the ground. The maiden took her sash and on instructions from George, bound the dragon with it. She was rewarded (by God), as this made the dragon calm and gentle. They led the dragon back down into the city. There was an ulterior motive to this scheme, George told the people of the city if they wanted him to kill the dragon, they must abandon worship of their false gods and follow Christianity. The people agreed and George lopped off the dragon's head. Everyone was baptised and a church was built.

St George's Dragon magical characteristics: Calming, binding, spirituality

Sigurd and Fáfnir

From Old Norse comes the myth of Sigurd and the dragon
Fáfnir, versions of the story can be found in old Icelandic texts
and mentions in many Norse poems.[41] The hero Sigurd was given
a sword by Regin, it was created from pieces of a sword owned
by Sigurd's father. The sword was called Gram and proved to be
strong and aided Sigurd in many battles. Regin told Sigurd of a
huge hoard of wealth guarded by a dragon but the only way to
get it was to kill the dragon. Regin advised Sigurd to dig a trench
and lay in wait for the dragon, when it came past, he was to stab
his sword upwards to kill it. Sigurd began to dig his ditch and as
he was doing so an old man appeared and suggested digging two
ditches, one to hide in and one for the dragon's blood to flow into.

Not long after he had finished digging, the dragon arrived,
as the huge bulk of the dragon's body stretched over the trench,
Sigurd struck his sword upwards. As he pushed with all his
strength the sword went into the dragon, along with the hilt and
then his arm, as he pulled it out, he was covered in blood.

Fáfnir felt the wound and began to writhe and lash about for
some time until he finally lay still. Sigurd jumped out from his
trench and faced the dragon, Fáfnir's life was slipping away and
just before the end he asked the name of his killer and who had
instructed him to do the deed.

Sigurd replied with his name and that he was going to claim
the dragon's hoard. Fáfnir advised that his hoard of gold would
be the death of Sigurd and the life of anyone who owned it
afterwards.

At this point Regin appeared and drank some of Sigurd's
blood, then instructed him to roast the heart of the dragon and
give it to him to eat. As the heart was cooking, Sigurd tasted
some of the blood that was seeping out to see if it was ready. As
he did so he suddenly understood the birds that were singing
nearby, they told him that Regin was going to kill him.

Sigurd listened and then drew his sword, cutting off Regin's head. Then he ate the dragon's heart himself and took all the hoard of treasure. Sadly, the prophecy from Fáfnir came true, Sigurd's life was full of misery and woe and he was eventually killed. Those that took his life fell foul of violence and greed until they were killed themselves.

Fáfnir's magical characteristics: Wealth, curses, understanding, greed

The Welsh Dragon

Although only officially adopted in 1959 as a national symbol, the red dragon has had Welsh connections for much longer.[42] Let's start with the Saxons as they advanced across ancient Briton and their King, Vortigern. He was attempting to build a castle on Mount Snowdon (North Wales) but each time they laid foundations the earth shook and tore the stones apart. Vortigern consulted a council of wizards who advised him to seek a boy born without a father, kill him and offer his blood to the ground. Eventually a young boy was found in the city of Carmarthen, his name was Merlin Ambrosius. He was summoned to the King who told him of his fate. Merlin was not having any of this and asked to speak to the wizards. He suggested the soil was dug below the foundation stones to see what was beneath. On doing so a pool of water was discovered. Merlin declared this to be the problem with the foundations falling apart. He suggested the pool of water was drained because he believed they would find two caves below. His prediction was proved to be the truth. As they watched the caves being unearthed, two dragons emerged, one was white, the other red. They fought each other with flames bellowing out. Eventually the white dragon won over the red dragon and pushed it to one side. However, the red dragon mustered the last of its strength and fought back to overcome the white dragon. King Vortigern was interested to know the symbolism of this battle, and Merlin provided him with a reason. He said the red dragon represented the Britons and the white dragon was the Saxons. And although the Saxons occupied much of Britain he predicted would eventually be chased back to their homeland.

This is just one version of the tale, but all of them follow a similar meaning.

Welsh Dragon magical characteristics: Valour, victory, predictions, truth, vengeance

Part III

Dragonology

Types of Dragons

*It's a metaphor of human bloody existence, a dragon. And
if that wasn't bad enough, it's also a bloody great hot flying
thing.* — Terry Pratchett

Describing the types of dragons from across the globe would
be a whole book in itself. I have given some of them here, but
this list is by no means complete. There will be different species
dependent on the area you live in but as a general rule most
dragons fall into one of the elemental categories of earth, air,
fire or water. Some cultures assign types of dragons to nature;
such as thunder, storms and winds. What I have tried to do here
is show how you can work with these specific dragons and what
magic they can help you with. These are my own deductions
drawn from learning about each dragon, by reading the myths
and legends of each one. I look at the stories and what the main
themes are, then I look at the landscape, the habitat and the
appearance of each dragon. All this information leads me to
the characteristics and magical energies of each one. I highly
recommend you research dragons in your local area and/or
country you live in and learn about them.

Amphiptere

A two-winged legless serpent often with colourful feathers on its
wings or sometimes leathery bat like wings, long spiked barbed
tail, a beak and a lindwurm type body. It has two tongues,
one normal and one that is arrow shaped with a venomous
bite. Found in many sizes from a foot long to enormous beasts.
The Amphiptere is often used in European heraldry and can be
found across Europe, Africa, Asia and the Americas. In Egypt
the frankincense trees are said to be guarded by Amphipteres.

Amphiptere magical characteristics: Communication, languages, gossip, protection

Gwiber

The name 'gwiber' comes from the route word meaning 'viper' so the gwiber is a serpent type dragon, although this one has wings. These are the Welsh variety of amphipteres. The gwiber doesn't usually breathe fire, instead it has a bite full of venom. The gwiber was believed to be created if a serpent managed to drink the milk of a nursing woman, causing it to grow into the gwiber. An interesting twist to the tale of gwibers, in all the legends they are only ever killed by peasants, shepherds or farmers, but never by a knight or king.

Gwiber magical characteristics: Wisdom, transformation

Basilisk & Cockatrice

Believed to be created by a rooster laying an egg (think about that for a moment), that is then incubated by a snake or a toad. Smaller in size to most other dragon types, the basilisk has the added skill of being able to kill people or animals with a single look, unless it was faced by a weasel, which apparently is immune to the death stare. It takes the form of a snake-like beast with a small crest on its head. A basilisk can be killed by seeing its own reflection in a mirrored surface or from hearing a cock crowing at dawn. In the bestiaries from the Dark Ages, the basilisk is described as a tiny serpent with a crest upon its head.[43] Later on in history the image changed to a lizard body with a rooster's head. Most common depictions describe a large rooster body with the tail of a lizard. These latter forms of the basilisk are known as a cockatrice.

Basilisk magical characteristics: Clarity, psychic abilities, vanity

Cockatrice magical characteristics: Clarity, psychic abilities, adaptability, transitions

Salamander

A small dragon shaped in the form of a lizard. This creature is totally fire-proof and able to live inside a fire with no worries about being harmed. The salamander is able to spit a poisonous foam from its mouth that causes the poor victim to lose their hair followed by their skin shrivelling, and then death. The flesh of a salamander is toxic to any person or animal that had an inclination to eat it, except for the pig. The pig can eat a salamander without any ill effects, but to be fair, pigs will eat anything. If a salamander pops into a lake or pond for a swim, the entire water system becomes poisoned. A salamander also has weaving skills, being able to create itself a cocoon from a fire-proof wool like material. This fire-proof wool was sought after by kings and emperors which was spun into cloth. The clothes created from it were thrown into the fire when they needed cleaning.

Salamander magical characteristics: Fire magic, creativity, protection

Pyrausta/Pyrallis

Seen as a fairy dragon, this is the smallest of the dragon species and resembles a variety of insects. It is believed to be a close relative of the salamander. The pyrausta has moth or butterfly wings, four limbs and large black eyes. Typically found in the furnaces of Cyprus where they would dance around in the flames, but also found in nature and woodlands.

Pyrausta/Pyrallis magical characteristics: Transformation, creativity, fire magic, nature magic

Eastern Dragons

Stories of dragons from the Far East, Asia, China and India are some of the oldest recorded. A lot of these dragons represent the weather or protect and control bodies of water. The breath of these dragons connected with the air to form rain. The eggs of these dragons look like rich beautiful jewels, being born as a small snake like creature and taking hundreds, sometimes thousands of years to reach maturity. A young Eastern dragon is called a kiao which has the form of a lindorm. Eventually it grows to become a lung and then a few hundred years later it transforms into a khoi-lung which is probably the most recognisable of the Eastern dragons and finally reaching adulthood it is known as a ying-lung resembling a beautifully ornate type of firedrake.

Chinese, Japanese and Korean dragons usually represent positive energy in the form of protection, life giving, prosperity and good fortune. These creatures are powerful but generally benevolent, and can be called upon to bring rain for good crops and respond to requests for help. Most of these dragons are associated with water in some form and they have a tradition of Dragon Kings. The Dragon Kings are thought to come down from the skies, out from the caves and up from beneath the waters every spring to bring new life and growth. Then they all fly up to the heavens to report on what they have done to the Supreme Ruler. The Dragon of the Heavens guards the home of the gods and creates wind and rain. The Dragon of the Earth creates the bases for rivers, streams and lakes. A further dragon lies under the earth looking after treasure hoards. Five Dragon Kings live under the sea in palaces made from crystal. Four Dragon Kings watch over rivers and many less important dragons guard lakes and water falls. The Chinese dragons are usually depicted with beautiful scales and flowing bodies. It has appeared with various types of head such as that of a horse, camel and tiger, usually with a serpent type body and often with long whiskers.

Japanese dragons are called tatsu. Similar in looks to a Chinese dragon but they only have three claws on each food where the Chinese has four. Japanese dragons live in the mountains, lakes, rivers and the seas. The tatsu controls the fish population and the allowance of fishing it gives to humans. Tsunamis and earthquakes are caused by angry Japanese dragons. Japanese dragons hatch from jewelled eggs but grow quickly into enormous beasts. Some tatsu dragons may form wings later on, bird like in appearance, in this form they are called hai riyo.

Eastern Dragon magical characteristics: Water magic, weather magic, abundance, prosperity, protection, good fortune

Lung/Long

A Chinese long scaly serpentine dragon with four legs, enormous eyes and long hair. Sometimes created from the parts of other animals. The name has been suggested to translate as 'high' or 'highest' giving the Lung a connection to the skies or perhaps the divine heavens. This connection seems to have developed into the Lung dragon being associated strongly with the clouds, particularly when they bring rain, and then onto water in all forms such as rivers and oceans. Rain rituals from the 6th century involved dragon imagery.

Lung Dragon magical characteristics: Dream work, weather magic, divine connection

Nāga

The Nāga dragon can be found in India and resembles a snake. The term nāga translates as 'serpent'. Some Nāga's have multiple heads and are often seen with golden flame like crowns on them. Some Nāga are half divine beings, half human or half cobra. The nāga lives in an underground kingdom filled with beautiful palaces. They were sent to the underground world by the Hindu god Brahma when their population became too many on earth. The nāgas are known to guard treasure and are often associated with different forms of water. In Buddhism the nāga is often found as a guardian of doorways.

Nāga magical characteristics: Underworld connection, water magic, prosperity, Otherworld portals, protection

Druk

A dragon from Tibetan and Bhutanese history, he is a thunder dragon with elaborate scales. Its body is long and thin and created with beautiful bright colours, often red and orange. The Druk lays its eggs in snow. The Druk appears on the Bhutan flag holding jewels to represent wealth. The Druk brings the ability to tell if people are lying and can communicate ideas and inspiration. This dragon can help humans to gain clarity and insight and bring with them wisdom and good fortune.

Druk magical characteristics: Truth, communication, clarity, wisdom, good fortune, wealth, inspiration

Egyptian Dragons

Ancient Egypt has its fair share of dragon tales most of which often seem to fall around the gods; the sun god, Ra, the storm god Set and Apophis/Apep a serpent who lives in the dark waters of the Underworld. The stories focus on the dragon being a creator or one that brings chaos, there is a definite divide, sometimes the dragon brings fertility other times it is pictured as a great enemy.

Egyptian dragon magical characteristics: Chaos, Underworld connection, creation, creativity, fertility

Guivres

This dragon hails from French medieval times. It emerged from the river Seine in 520CE. The guivres has a long reptilian neck, slender snout and jaws, heavy brows, horns, membranous wings and toxic disease laden breath. The guivres also spouts jets of water. They are known to be very aggressive, however, they do seem to be fearful of naked humans. Apparently, the sight of a human without clothing would make them turn away. The Guivres likes to live in woodlands or forests as long as there is a source of water and the landscape is damp.

Guivres magical characteristics: Water magic, warrior energy

Heraldic or Drake

Known as the Heraldic or sometimes Drake, this is probably the most recognised form of dragon. Huge and covered in tough scales, with two bat like wings and four legs, ending in clawed talons. A horse shaped head often with horns and large teeth along with hypnotic eyes. This dragon also has a long tail ridged with spines and usually a spike or fork on the end. This is the type of dragon St. George and countless other heroes battle with in stories.

In the original stories the Drake was immortal, in more modern tales you find it difficult to kill but not impossible. Each Drake would have a vulnerable spot somewhere about its body, different places on each dragon. Drakes are also known to be accomplished shape shifters; they are also believed to be able to self-heal wounds. Some Drakes have the power to become invisible, speak many languages and change size from tiny to huge in a blink.

Drakes like to nest in rocky cliffs, deep caves, forests, lakes and seas. This type of dragon often encompasses all four of the elements.

From German and Norse mythology, there are two types of drake:

- The Cold Drake is blue or white in colour and can release ice through their mouths.
- Fire Drakes are warm coloured and breath fire, huge jets of flames that are hot enough to melt stone and rock. It is the firedrake that loves to hoard treasure.

Drake magical characteristics: Warrior energy, courage, vulnerability, shape shifting, healing, communication, the elements, prosperity, fire magic

Hydra

The hydra is a multi-headed dragon, quite often with three, seven or nine heads and in some sources, up to fifty. The hydra is a serpent type dragon with multiple limbs and wings that can re-grow if severed. The word 'hydra' is Greek and translates as 'water serpent'.

Hydra magical characteristics: Death and rebirth, renewal, growth, knowledge, water magic

Knucker

An English dragon found in the county of Sussex, the word 'knucker' translates as 'water monster'. The knucker is a long serpent with small wings, small head and leathery skin, oh and it has fangs. This creature seems to be particularly fond of shiny objects including glass. The knucker lives in a knuckerhole which is a deep pool of water.

Knucker magical characteristics: Hidden depths, mysteries, water magic, material wealth

Leviathan

From the Hebrew Bible, the Tanakh, Judaism, Christianity and Gnostic beliefs.[44] The leviathan is a sea dragon with several wings or fins and a strong tail. It is often described with several heads. Said to demonic and chaotic and to eat the souls of those who have been damned. In some cases, the Leviathan is used to represent the evils of the material world and corresponds to the seven deadly sins.

Leviathan magical characteristics: Chaos, material wealth, envy, jealousy

Western

Fire breathing dragons with six limbs, two large wings and long sharp claws. Sadly, the dragons from Western tales are usually portrayed as evil. They live in caves or mountains, and they like the cold and the dark. European and Mediterranean stories often include the dragon as a representation of negative energy, a sin or a vice of some kind and then a hero that slays them. These stories are all about conflict between good and evil. The dragon being chaos, destruction and death and the hero representing order, creation and life. Although there are many stories of Western dragons eating animals and humans, there are also tales where they have given assistance to travellers or provided protection for people, treasure hoards or sacred places. They are believed to be the holders of secrets, knowledge and power but to gain this you must first kill the dragon, drink its blood and eat the flesh. I do not advise this course of action, once you have built a relationship with a dragon, if you prove worthy the dragon will share its knowledge with you, without the need for bloodshed.

Western dragon magical characteristics: Conflict, chaos, death and rebirth, organisation, travel, protection, wealth, secrets, knowledge

Wyrm

A legless European creature resembling an enormous snake that spits poisonous gas or venom. The wyrm has hypnotic powers to lure victims in. The wyrm can also wind itself around its prey to crush them to death. The Wyrm is believed to be able to regrow any section of their body that was severed. This type of dragon is particularly fond of milk. They live in caves by water and have a tendency to hoard treasure. Both wyrms and lindwurms are gigantic in size, big enough to wrap themselves around entire mountains several times. When a sea wyrm grows large enough, its body is so heavy that it drags it down beneath the waves to live on the sea bed.

Wyrm magical characteristics: Clarity, psychic abilities, binding, healing, renewal, prosperity, sea magic

Lindwurm/Lindorm

Similar to wyrms in that they have serpentine bodies and scaly skin but they have two clawed front limbs. Lindwurms do not have wings. The name derives from old High German and translates as 'flexible dragon' or 'ensnaring serpent'. The lindwurm has a taste for eating corpses and often frequents graveyards for a snack. The skin shed from a lindwurm has magical properties and can increase your knowledge about nature and medicinal herbs.

Lindwurm magical characteristics: Flexibility, transitions, changes, knowledge, herbals, nature magic, releasing

Wyvern

Very similar in description and characteristics to the Heraldic dragon, the Wyvern only has two legs as opposed to four. Their heads tend to be more snake like, and they often have longer necks. Legs of the Wyvern are bird like with large, curved talons. Their tails are finished with a diamond or arrow shape tip which carries a sting that can kill. Some wyverns breathe fire, but others have breath that is foul and usually toxic. The name Wyvern comes from Middle English and translates as 'snake' or 'viper'. The Wyvern does love the role of guardian over treasure hoards. Outbreaks of plagues and illness were usually blamed on the wyvern. They appear to be smaller than most Drakes, and do not seem to have the same magical powers, but still very formidable.

Wyvern magical characteristics: Gossip, prosperity, cleansing, purification, striking action

Zmey/Żmij

Zmey is a Slavic dragon often seen with multiple heads that breathe fire.[45] His body is covered with red or green scales and he has iron claws. The name translates to mean 'viper'. Zmey have a connection to the god of the lowlands, magic and the underworld. They are very smart and known to be tricksters and shape shifters. The Zmey has a leaning towards seducing human woman and their offspring are believed to become great warriors. Zmey can also become protectors of villages when storms hit.

Zmey magical characteristics: Magic, the underworld, trickery, shape shifting, cunning, protection

Part IV

Dragon Magic

Dragon Magic

No, I would not want to live in a world without dragons, as I
would not want to live in a world without magic, for that is a
world without mystery, and that is a world without faith.
— R.A. Salvatore

In this section of the book, I will share with you how I work
with dragons and their magic. Your journey and experiences
will not be exactly the same as mine, but hopefully this will
give you a starting point. Remember this is about forming and
building a relationship, you will need to put time and effort
into it just as you would with any relationship. Working with
dragons will probably be very different from any other energy
you have experienced. It is very rare for a dragon to approach
you out of the blue, generally they only respond if we invite
them to work with us. Always remember your manners and be
polite, these are ancient creatures that deserve our respect.

Do not expect to see information in this book that is light and
airy. My experience with dragons and dragon magic is one of
power, strength and hard work. Dragons are ancient, they are
primordial and do not tolerate being summoned nor do they
appreciate any half-hearted lack of commitment.

You might ask why a large part of this introductory book is
taken up with origin stories and mythology on dragons. The
answer is, because it is important to know and understand
these things about dragons BEFORE you begin to work with
them.

We can work with dragons for many things. Once a
relationship has been formed you can ask a dragon to assist with
your spell work, divination and to bring their energy to a ritual,
they may also be happy enough to become your guardian.

How to Summon a Dragon

Do not. Never summon a dragon, seriously don't do it. Dragons will not respond well to being summoned. Dragons are ancient, they are wise, majestic and powerful. Summoning them will either annoy them greatly, for which you will be made to pay or they will completely ignore you because of your arrogance and insolence. They will, however, respond if you ask them politely using respect and manners. Working with dragons is the same as any other relationship with a mentor or teacher. You will need to work hard to build trust and communication, just as you would with any other relationship. Treat dragons with the utmost respect and always be mindful of your manners. They are not there to be ordered around, toyed with or treated badly, not that they would respond to any of that kind of nonsense anyway.

Guardian Dragons

My fire dragon is my guardian dragon and has been with me for many years. I am very grateful to be able to work with him and benefit from his energy and support. You may find once you begin your dragon journey that a guardian dragon finds you straight away. Or it may take some time, it will depend on each individual and what works best for your situation. You do not make the choice, the dragon does. Guardian dragons do need some attention, you can't just ignore them for months and then expect them to rock up when you need them to. They will get bored with lack of attention and wander off, and quite frankly I wouldn't blame them. This is where an altar works well because you can spend some time at it on a regular basis, lighting a flame, giving offerings or just making a connection. Meditation is also a good route for maintaining a relationship. Your Guardian Dragon will become your best friend, they will know what you are thinking, often before you even do. They will be able to offer advice, guidance and support along with protection if and when needed. They will be honest and direct and you will not always like what they have to say, it won't always be what you want to hear, but it will be what you need. It pays to learn to trust them and follow their direction. A Dragon Guardian can also help boost your confidence by stepping up to stand beside you when needed.

Dragon Guidance

He had turned into a dragon while he was asleep. Sleeping on a dragon's hoard with greedy, dragonish thoughts in his heart, he had become a dragon himself. — C.S. Lewis

Whilst your Guardian Dragon is always with you, there are times when other dragons may come forward with specific messages or guidance for particular projects or issues happening in your life. It might be that you have a problem and sit down to meditate to gain some insight and a dragon comes forward to assist. You may be out and about and feel the presence of dragon energy, stop and listen for any messages. This type of dragon connection is usually fleeting, they may just be there to impart one short communication. If you are working with something specific the dragon may appear to walk beside you for the duration of the project, providing you with insight and guidance as you go. Be open to whatever comes your way or makes itself known to you, there will be a reason for it.

Meditation

One of the easiest ways to connect with dragon energy is to meditate. I know it is often the answer given for everything, but meditation opens up a doorway to another realm and puts your subconscious into a more open and receptive form.

Make yourself comfortable in a place where you will not be disturbed. Light some incense and put on some plinky plonky music if you wish. Close your eyes.

Begin a count down, slowly from 10 to 1.

As your world dissipates you find yourself at the foot of a mountain. The lower slopes are grassy and lush and the top disappears into the skies. Feel the sun and the slight breeze on your skin and breathe in the fresh air.

You start to make your way up the gentle slope, feeling the soft springy grass under your feet, until you see a glimpse of slate grey rocks ahead.

As you walk closer you see that the rocks form a cave in the side of the slope.

Something catches your eye on the rocks framing the cave mouth. Stepping closer you notice symbols carved into the rock face. What shapes are they, do any of them seem familiar to you? Are you drawn to any specific image or symbol?

You are drawn to step just inside the opening of the cave mouth. The air is cool inside the cave and it smells a little musty.

A large flat boulder is set just inside and you sit down upon it, facing the darkness inside the cave.

You sit quietly listening for a moment, as there are faint sounds coming from deep within the depths.

Something is heading towards you, but you do not feel afraid.

Slowly a creature begins to emerge from the dark until you can see it quite clearly. It stops just in front you and you get an overwhelming sense of peace.

Do not use words, but send your request via thought to the dragon. Make the request that you would like to build a relationship with it and open lines of communication. Be sure to ask politely and mention that you wish to learn from its wisdom.

Wait patiently, it may take some time for the response to come.

Once the dragon has given you its reply, if the option is there, ask any further questions that you feel are necessary.

When you are finished, ask the dragon if it requires anything from you.

After the dragon has replied, thank it for its time and energy and bid your farewell.

You may now stand and make your way back out of the cave. Take a last look at the symbols and images carved into the stone and make a mental note of the ones that resonated with you.

Carefully make your way back down the slope back to where you began your journey.

Slowly count up from 10 back to 1.

Gently come back to this reality, wriggling your fingers and toes and open your eyes.

You may want to jot down any of the main symbols and images you saw for further investigation. Eat and drink something.

If the dragon gave permission to start building a relationship, you can come back to this meditation regularly until you have built your own scenario and connection with it. The dragon may not be willing to be a guardian, if this is the case you can use this meditation to come back to in the future. You may find that a different dragon greets you on your next visit.

Dragon Flight

Once you have built a good relationship with your dragon, they may grant you permission to go on a flight with them. The experience of flying on a dragon is a very special one, it can provide you with insight and clarity in ways you would not expect.

Make yourself comfortable in a place where you will not be disturbed. Light some incense and put on some plinky plonky music if you wish. Close your eyes.

Begin a count down, slowly from 10 to 1.

As your world dissipates you find yourself at the foot of a mountain. The lower slopes are grassy and lush and the top disappears into the skies. Feel the sun and the slight breeze on your skin and breathe in the fresh air.

As you look around the landscape you hear a noise far above you, very faint but it is loud enough to grab your attention.

Looking up towards the skies you see a small dot, as you watch the shape grows larger.

Then you can make out the shape of a dragon, flying majestically through the air, making its way down towards you.

Eventually it lands on the grass a short way from you. You feel the ground beneath your feet shudder slightly as it alights.

You nod with respect towards the dragon and ask permission to approach, the large beast returns your nod.

Once you are beside the dragon it invites you to join it for a flight, and lowers its body close to the ground allowing you to climb up.

You make yourself as comfortable as possible, sitting just behind the dragon's head and in front of its wings.

Slowly and gently the dragon begins to move forward along the ground and you hold on tightly. Then suddenly it lifts off, heading upwards.

You feel the rush of adrenaline and the breeze hits your face as the dragon climbs higher and higher into the skies.

Up, up, up!

You pass through a drift of wispy clouds and the dragon levels out just above them.

The feeling of flight and being so high up is thrilling.

You continue to hold tightly as the dragon follows the air currents, when you feel ready you take a look over the side and watch the landscape spread out below you. What can you see? What landmarks can you make out?

Up in front of you a large cliff top begins to appear and the dragon seems to be heading for it. As it reaches the top, the dragon slowly begins to descend, landing gently on a flat outcrop.

You catch your breath and then climb down onto the ground.

The dragon gestures for you to sit fairly close to the edge of the cliff, and joins you, sitting beside you.

You feel the urge to ask questions of the dragon and it listens, then it responds.

The dragon also encourages you to take a look across the landscape from a perspective that you might not be used to. You are high above everything on the cliff top, a view that most do not get to see. The dragon asks you to see your problems, issues and queries from that different view point.

You look, you ask questions, you listen...

When you are ready the dragon lowers itself down enabling you to climb back up onto its back.

Gently it begins to move across the ground and then takes flight.

Up, up, up!

Passing back up through the bank of clouds and then levelling out.

You think about the advice and insight the dragon provided you as you glide through the skies.

Eventually the dragon begins a slow descent, back down through the clouds and finally landing gently on the grass.

You are back at the base of the mountain where you began your journey.

The dragon lowers itself once more enabling you to climb carefully down.

You turn and hug the dragon and thank it for the experience and the advice.

You watch as the dragon turns and once more takes flight, gradually heading off into the distance.

Slowly count up from 10 back to 1.

Gently come back to this reality, wriggling your fingers and toes and open your eyes.

You may want to jot down any of the main symbols and images you saw for further investigation. Eat and drink something.

Seeing Dragons

In my experience people do not often see a clear image of a dragon, at least at first. You might be out in the woods or on a nature walk and get a 'feeling' a prickling sensation that something is there. That feeling may happen continually on and off over the next few weeks or months. Occasionally, particularly when you are outside in nature you might see a glimmer of something, a blurring on the landscape. Very rarely will you see a huge almighty dragon in full high-definition technicolour right in front of you. For a start, most dragons are quite large and there probably is not the space in your living room for it to fit comfortably. Outside where there is room, a dragon will not show itself randomly, because it takes a lot of trust for it to do so. Do not discount any of those moments when you know something is around you. When you feel confident to do so, ask if it would like to make a connection with you, tell it that you are open to dragon communication. Once a connection has been made and you start to build a relationship, using meditation and some of the suggestions within this book, then you may get a clearer picture of your dragon. Do not forget your other senses, use them as well, what do you hear and what do you smell?

Dragon Names and Gender

Come not between the dragon, and his wrath.
— William Shakespeare

Having worked with many dragons over the years I must confess, I have never known any of their names. And although I have gotten the feeling of which gender each one is, for instance I am fairly sure my Guardian fire dragon is a male, I haven't known for sure about that either. Basically, I am saying, to ask about the name or gender of a dragon seems a bit of a taboo subject. My recommendation would be to not ask. If at any point the dragon feels the need to tell you then take it as a great sign of respect and be mindful of your manners when addressing them. But that last part is always a good idea anyway.

Note: After writing about the gender of my fire dragon in this book manuscript, later that evening I got the overwhelming feeling he was present. The energy was different, not masculine but a strong feminine energy for the first time ever, along with amusement. I still believe my guardian fire dragon is male, but he was showing me that all creatures have both energies within them. It was a poignant reminder to me.

Altars

Dragons do like to be honoured, and having an altar set up just for them is an excellent way to help make and maintain a connection. And, of course, to stroke their ego. If you are short on space then a candle specifically dedicated to dragon energy will do, but if you have room, then an altar just for dragons goes a long way. It does not need to be fancy or elaborate, unless you want it to be.

My suggestions for your dragon altar are below, but as always trust your intuition and your budget. Also listen to your dragon, there may be specific things they want you to include on the altar.

Offering bowl for milk – just a small dish will work, give regular offerings of milk, but make sure to clean the bowl each time and do not leave the milk out for days at a time. Sour milk smells bad to you and to the dragon.

Candle – most dragons, even the non-fire breathing ones appreciate a flame. Having a dedicated candle for dragon energy works very well. Light the candle each day and honour dragon energy. The flame can also be used to focus dragon energy and for you to make a connection.

Ornaments – there is a huge array of dragon ornaments on the market, from small jewellery charms to garden size statues. Obviously, the space you have will dictate what you use. Keep an eye out in charity/thrift stores for bargains. I have several; a small curled ceramic dragon that fits into the palm of my hand that I hold when I meditate, when not in use it sits on my altar. I also have colourful clay figures, and detailed cast images, all fairly small. You can often find candle holders and chalices that are decorated with dragons too. If you are creative then you could make your own from air dry clay or coloured modelling clay. Painted images of dragons on canvas or pebbles and embroidered dragon designs on fabric also work well.

Pictures – there are some incredibly talented artists out there who depict dragons in their artwork. Whilst the images can be printed from the internet, I would encourage you to purchase direct from the artist if you can. Most artists produce small prints or postcards of their work that are inexpensive.

Crystals – there are a number of crystals associated with dragon energy (I have included some suggestions within this book) but use crystals that you are drawn to.

Coins – a lot of dragons love treasure, so it makes sense to pop a few coins on your altar. Whilst it will not constitute a hoard, it is a nod in the right direction. Old pieces of jewellery that sparkle also work well.

Incense – there is no smoke without fire, burning incense on your dragon altar will help put you in the right space but also honour the dragon, particularly if you select a corresponding scent.

Altar cloth – placing a cloth on the altar can add in some colour magic, it can also be used to correspond with the elements.

If you find a piece of cloth with a dragon image on then that would work wonderfully. It is also practical and protects your furniture from oils and wax.

Cauldron – I like to have a cauldron or fire-proof dish of some sort on my dragon altar, this is useful for burning any petitions safely, it can also be filled with water for scrying.

Cleansing and Consecrating Your Altar

Start by cleansing your altar space, before you add anything to it. This just clears away any negative energy that might be lurking. Then I like to consecrate the space, this is a method that helps dedicate the altar for your purpose. You literally tell the space it is sacred to dragons and dragon energy.

To cleanse the altar I use incense smoke, choose a scent that resonates with you. I like to use bundles of dried herbs from my garden, something like garden sage, rosemary and lavender. Light the bundle or incense stick and waft the smoke across the altar surface and then into any corners. I find it also works well to waft the smoke specifically to each of the four compass quarters. Say something like:

With this smoke I cleanse and clear
Negative energy disperse from here

Next you need to consecrate the altar, I like to do this with an essential oil blend, but you could use salt or water if you prefer.

Dragon Altar Consecration Oil Blend

10ml base oil – olive oil
Olive is ruled by the Sun and corresponds to the elements of fire and air, olive brings integrity, passion, protection and spirituality.

5 drops cinnamon essential oil (not just because it is one of my favourites)
Cinnamon is ruled by the Sun and aligns with the element of fire it brings the magic of changes, focus, power, protection and spirituality.

10 drops dragon's blood essential oil, it had to be really, didn't it?
Dragon's blood aligns with the element of fire and brings power, protection and, of course, dragon magic.

5 drops ginger essential oil
Ginger is a fire element oil and brings the magic of power, protection and is excellent for consecrating.

5 drops pine essential oil
Pine is a fire and air element oil and brings the magic of focus, protection, purification, truth and dragon energy.

Stand in front of your empty altar space, place your hands, palms down onto the altar surface and say:

Now I consecrate this altar as a sacred space
A place to commune and connect with the dragon race
Ancient energies to support and protect
Dragon lines converge and connect

Now take a dab of your consecration oil on your finger and dab each corner of the altar surface and then in the centre. You can repeat the chant at each point if you would like to. If you prefer you can add essential oil to water in a spritzer bottle and use it as a spray over the altar rather than an oil blend.

Once your dragon altar is consecrated you can place your magical tools and items onto it. As I position them, I like to state out loud their purpose and dedicate each piece to dragon energy, this can be done by dabbing them with your consecrating oil blend if you wish.

Altar and the Elements

If you work with the elements and would like to bring the qualities of dragon elementals into your sacred space you can place items on the altar that correspond. If you can find items decorated with dragons then even better, but simple tools or symbols will also work. Even natural pebbles painted with the elemental triangles on can be used.

> Earth – Pebbles and stones, twigs, leaves, a dish of soil or salt
> Air – Feathers, incense
> Fire – Candles, a knife or an athame
> Water – Chalice or cup, dish of water, shells, sea glass

As you place each element item onto your altar state out loud its purpose, you can call in the elemental energy of dragon for each one if you wish.

Dragons of earth, ancient and old
Bring stability and guidance so bold

Dragons of air, flight and free
Bring intuition and clarity to me

Dragons of fire, sparks and flame
Bring passion and creativity to the game

Dragons of water, oceans and sea
Bring control of emotions now to me

Dragon Candles

I confess, I do not make my own candles from scratch. I have attempted to but found it to be a messy business. I do, however, like to decorate and personalise bought candles. I find this not only adds my own energy to them but allows me to dedicate candles for specific purpose. Candles work wonderfully in dragon magic and I have one on my altar specifically for working with dragon energy.

Be mindful: Never leave a candle burning unattended. Adding oils and herbs to your candle can cause the flame to sputter and flare.

This is what I use for my main general dragon candle:

- A large pillar candle, usually in a fiery colour such as red, orange or sassy pink.
- Essential oil blend such as the consecration blend given in this book, or simply plain olive oil.
- Crushed herb blend which consists of Pine needles and Dragon's blood resin

First, I cleanse the candle using incense smoke. Then I consecrate it for dragon energy. I hold the candle in my hands and close my eyes. I focus on visualising dragons and connecting with their energy. I say:

Dragon energy, powerful and strong
For my dragon connection to belong
Magic of dragons I honour thee
This candle is your connection to me

I then dress the candle with the essential oil, using my fingers to cover the candle in the oil, drawing it down from the top of the candle to the bottom. Next, I roll the candle in the crushed herb mixture so that it sticks to the outside surface. Then I repeat the chant and place the candle in a safe holder and pop it on my altar. I light this candle every day in honour of dragons and their magic and to allow me to speak to them direct if I need to.

If I want to bring in the energy of one of the elemental dragons, or use the candles in ritual for the quarters this is what I use:

Earth Dragon Candle:
Brown or green candle
Sesame or avocado oil as both are ruled by earth
Crushed sesame seeds or oats

Air Dragon Candle:
Yellow or white candle
Almond oil as it is ruled by the element of air
Crushed dried mint leaves

Fire Dragon Candle:
Red or orange candle
Sunflower oil as it is ruled by the element of fire
Dragon's blood resin or cinnamon

Water Dragon Candle:
Blue candle
Coconut oil as it is ruled by the element of water
Crushed dried thyme leaves

I dress each candle with the oil and roll in crushed herbs as I do with the main dragon candle. You can use the element chants that I gave for dressing your altar as you create each element candle.

Offerings

As you work with dragons and their energy it is advisable to give offerings to them for their help and support, it is after all, only good manners. I cannot stress enough that this is a relationship and there needs to be a balance. You cannot keep asking for help, support or a dragon to lend energy to your spell work or rituals without giving them something in return. They may ask for something specific from you and it may be in the form of a physical offering but it could also be your time dedicated to a task or a song, dance or poem for them. Listen to their needs and also trust your intuition about what to give as an offering. I have already mentioned how much most dragons love milk but they also seem to like sparkly things such as coins and pretty crystals, it is a hoarding thing! I find the offerings are part of building and maintaining the relationship. I do not make offerings as such to my friends to keep the relationship with them but I do make time for them, help and support them when they need it and, of course, buy them coffee and cake on occasion too. Your dragon relationship works in a similar way, but it is probably wiser to leave an offering of milk on your altar for your dragon than take it out to the local café for a coffee.

Elemental Dragons

In my experience most dragons align with one of the elements in some way. Dragons obviously have their own unique and individual personalities and characteristics, but you will usually find some vein of an element in each one. Elemental dragons carry strong energies for the element they correspond with. Elemental dragons can turn up in all kinds of situations, you may find one becomes your Guardian (as with myself and my fire dragon), they work well for lending their energy to spell working and brilliantly in ritual to represent the four quarters.

Earth Dragons

Bring all the qualities the element of earth and are often associated with mountains and forests.

Positive Qualities – Abundance, Prosperity, Fertility, Grounding, Employment, Stability, endurance, tolerance, patience, planning, career, selfishness, practicality, responsibility, sensuality, strength, tolerance, fertility, wealth, wisdom, potential, reaping, sowing, humility, responsibility, tolerance, practicality

Negatives – depression, domineering, greed, attention seeking, laziness, melancholy, stubbornness

Air Dragons

Bring all the qualities the element of air and are often associated with storms and weather patterns.

Positive Qualities – Intellect, travel, instruction, study, knowledge, finding lost items, illumination

Negatives – Theft, nerves, indecision, insecurity, anxiety, impulsive, paranoia, prejudice

Fire Dragons

Bring all the qualities of the element of fire and are often associated with volcanoes, desert and arid places.

Positive Qualities – Courage, change, energy, protection, strength, passion, personal power, ingenuity, manifesting, will power, bravery, beginnings, drive, action, death and rebirth, movement, ideas, change, sensuality, purification, breaking bad habits, authority, banishing, transformation, negativity, sex, authority, speed, creativity, destruction, cleansing, sexuality, force, motion, anger, desire, work, freedom

Negatives – Anger, jealousy, stubbornness, greed, arrogance, resentment, possessiveness, cruelty, violence

Water Dragons

Bring all the qualities the element of water and are often associated with oceans, rivers and lakes.

Positive Qualities – Purification, love, relationships, dreams, peace, compassion, emotions, nurturing, death, psychic abilities, sexuality, trust

Negative Qualities – Fear, jealousy, hatred, deceit, sorrow, spite, treachery

Spirit Dragons

Spirit dragons are extremely helpful for all kinds of psychic work. They can also provide a connection to the divine, help with your spirituality, connections of all kinds, value and personal growth. The spirit element does not have the same correspondence ideas as the other elements as it is not physical. Spirit is a conduit between the physical and spiritual realms.

Chaos Dragon

Although not an elemental dragon as such, the chaos dragon does need a mention because he appears often. The chaos dragon is often seen as negative and evil, but that is not the case. What he does bring is chaos obviously, in the form of destruction. However, this destruction does destroy and often levels things completely, but it brings change, necessary change. In order to have re-birth and renewal you need destruction first. Chaos Dragon brings about transformation usually on a grand scale. It can literally bring total chaos, but from that comes change and ultimately regeneration to bring about new ways, new thoughts and a better more positive outcome.

Positive Qualities – Change, transformation, death and rebirth, renewal, regeneration

Negative Qualities – Chaos!, unpredictable

Dragon Incense

I find that incense works well as an offering, particularly if you have spent some time creating the blend yourself with the intent of giving it as a dragon offering. Incense also creates a connection to dragon energy. These are loose incense blends to be used on a charcoal disc or warmed in the top of an oil burner. As a general guide I like to include a resin, a woody ingredient and then herbs and/or spices. The resin and wood part help the incense to burn for longer. I have given some of my own blend recipes aligned to the four elements but do experiment and see what works for you and your dragon. All of these have a dragon's blood base because it is all about the dragon!

Earth Dragon Incense
2 parts Dragon's blood resin
1 part mugwort
1 part peanut shells or dried grass
A few drops of patchouli essential oil

Air Dragon Incense
2 parts Dragon's blood resin
2 parts caraway seeds
1 part star anise
1 few drops of vanilla essential oil

Fire Dragon Incense
2 parts Dragon's blood resin
2 parts cinnamon bark
1 part coffee beans
A few drops frankincense essential oil

Water Dragon Incense
2 parts Dragon's blood resin
2 parts cardamom seeds
1 part heather flowers
A few drops geranium essential oil

Dragon Sigils

Working with sigils is an excellent source of extra power to add to your magical workings. I also use sigils to carve into candles that I dedicate to the dragons. They are particularly useful to use on petitions in spell working, the sigil can be added to the petition on top of your request or intent, thus adding extra dragon power. There are several ways of creating sigils but the easiest is using letters. Each sigil will be unique and personal to you.

You will need:

A piece of paper
A pen

First you need an intent and a phrase that sums up your intended outcome. To draw in the energy of dragon you can simply use the word 'DRAGON' or extend it to read 'DRAGON POWER'. My example here uses the phrase 'DRAGON POWER'.

We will use the letters of the phrase to create the sigil but we need to simplify it first by removing all the vowels and any letters that are duplicated, once you have done that you end up with:

'DRGNPW'

Now you need to grab a pen and paper and draw the letters, you can draw them one on top of another or you can space them out linking them together — be guided by your intuition and be as creative or as simple as you want. Create a pleasing image using the letters.

Once you have done that your sigil is complete. Your intent is in the letters, so you can bury it in the earth, burn it in the fire, wash it away in water — whatever works for you. This will release the energy into the Universe and kick start the sigil magic. If you are using it to dedicate a candle to dragons then the image can be carved into the side of the candle. If you are adding it to your dragon altar the sigil image can be traced onto the surface with water or oil, or recreate the sigil using sand, salt or flour.

Dragon Spells

Dragon energy can be called upon for any type of magic, just be mindful they will add energy in a way they feel is correct. It may affect the outcome of the spell in a way you might not expect. I have learnt to trust that dragons generally know best. I have given a couple of templates for spell workings here, each one can be used for the intents listed below, just use the corresponding options given for each one.

Basic Candle Magic Spell

You will need:

Candle in a corresponding colour, I recommend a spell candle or small rolled beeswax
Corresponding herbs
Corresponding oil blend
Pin or knife to carve
Candle holder
Slip of paper
Pen or pencil
Matches or lighter
Cauldron or fire-proof dish

Method:

- Charge the candle and each of the ingredients (herbs and oil) with your intent. Hold them in both hands and send energy into them. You can also ask your dragon to breathe the intent into the items as well.
- Carve your symbol/sigil into the side of the candle.
- Dress the candle with your essential oil blend.
- Roll the candle in your herb blend.
- Set the candle in a safe holder.
- Write your petition on the paper.
- Say our chant.
- Light the candle.
- Sit quietly and call upon your dragon to lend its magic and energy to your spell, tell it what your goal is, see your dragon working with you to achieve the desired outcome.
- Visualise your wishes and desires happening.

- Once the candle flame reaches the carved symbol take your petition and light it from the flame, say your chant and allow it to burn and drop it into the cauldron.
- The ashes can be buried or sent to the winds.

Basic Pouch Spell

You will need:

Square of fabric/felt and a ribbon or a drawstring pouch or an envelope in a corresponding colour
Corresponding herbs
Corresponding crystal chip or tumble stone
Slip of paper
Pen or pencil

Method:
- Charge your herbs and crystals with your intent. Hold them in both hands and send energy into them. You can also ask your dragon to breathe the intent into the items as well.
- Write your petition words, chant or draw a sigil onto your slip of paper.
- Drop the paper into your pouch and say your chant.
- Add a pinch of herbs to your pouch and repeat your chant.
- Add the crystal to your pouch and repeat your chant.
- Place the pouch in your bag or pocket or place it on your altar.

Strength

One of the most striking powers of a dragon is their strength. Physical strength, of course, but their strength to have endured and survived for such a long time despite what has been thrown at them. Use dragon magic to help you find your own inner strength.

Candle Spell for Strength
Candle colour: White, black, yellow, red
Herbs and Oils: Bay, black pepper, daisy, lavender, oak, sesame, sunflower, tea
Crystal: Agate, bloodstone, garnet, hematite, black obsidian, quartz, sunstone, tiger's eye, tourmaline
Petition words (or add your own sigil): Bring me strength
Chant: *Dragon power bring to me*
          Inner strength and energy for all to see
          Dragon roar, power within
          Strength of character now bring in

Power

There probably are not many creatures as powerful as a dragon. Draw upon that energy, with their permission, of course, to boost your own personal power and energy.

Candle Spell for Power
Candle colour: White, yellow, red, purple, gold
Essential oil blend:
Herbs: Bay, black pepper, cinnamon, coltsfoot, dragon's blood, echinacea, elm, ginger, oak, plantain, rowan
Crystal: Amber, bloodstone, orange calcite, malachite, black obsidian, sunstone, tourmaline
Petition words (or add your own sigil): Increase my personal power
Chant: *Dragon power bring to me*
          An energy boost for all to see
          Dragon roar, power within
          Personal power now bring in

Courage & Confidence

Lions are well known for their courageous roar, but have you ever compared that to the roar of a dragon? Let me tell you, the lion's roar is a mere squeak compared to that of a dragon. Dragon magic will help you with your own courage, generally in life or for a specific situation.

Candle Spell for Courage
Candle colour: White, orange, red
Herbs and Oils: Bay, benzoin, black pepper, daisy, fennel, lavender, myrrh, oak, olive, sesame, sunflower, tea, thyme, yarrow
Crystal: Agate, amethyst, green aventurine, carnelian, garnet, goldstone, labradorite, black obsidian, tiger's eye, tourmaline
Petition words (or add your own sigil): Bring me courage and confidence
Chant: *Dragon power bring to me*
            Courage and confidence for all to see
            Dragon roar, power within
            Personal courage now bring in

Manifesting

Dragons are well known for hoarding treasure, so who better to help you bring in your own? Work with your dragon to keep money rolling in and provide abundance of all kinds.

Candle Spell for Manifesting
Candle colour: White, green, gold, brown
Herbs and Oils: Basil, bergamot (orange), cedar, chamomile, cloves, cumin, dandelion, frankincense, ginger, grass, honeysuckle, jasmine, mint, mustard, nutmeg, patchouli, pine, poppy, rose, sage, sesame, sunflower, tea
Crystal: agate, amber, carnelian, citrine, garnet, goldstone, labradorite, malachite, smoky quartz, sunstone, tiger's eye
Petition words (or add your own sigil): Money/abundance/ prosperity come to me

Chant: *Dragon power bring to me*
        Money, prosperity and abundance to see
        Dragon roar, power within
        Manifest my wishes and now bring in

Healing

Dragons have a positive healing side to their nature, many of them have their own regeneration or self-healing aspects. We can ask them to help us for healing energy too.

Candle Spell for Healing
    Candle colour: White, blue, green, pink
    Herbs and Oils: Bay, blackthorn, cinnamon, coriander, fennel, ginger, juniper, lemon balm, lungwort, marjoram, mint, myrrh, nettle, oak, pine, rose, rosemary, rowan, thyme
    Crystal: Agate, green aventurine, bloodstone, citrine, fluorite, hematite, labradorite, moonstone, quartz, rose quartz, sunstone, tiger's eye
    Petition words (or add your own sigil): Healing energy and good health
    Chant: *Dragon power bring to me*
            Healing energy and good health to see
            Dragon roar, power within
            Healing magic now bring in

Protection

Need some protection? Who ya gonna call? Dragons, of course! A big ole beastie of a dragon will protect you against anything, you only have to look at a dragon to know you do not want to take it on.

Candle Spell for Protection
    Candle colour: White, black, blue, brown, red, silver

Herbs and Oils: Basil, bay, benzoin, black pepper, blackthorn, cardamom, chillies, cinnamon, clove, copal, cumin, dragon's blood, ginger, hawthorn, lemon, mint, mustard, nutmeg, pine, rose, rosemary, sage, salt, star anise, yarrow

Crystal: Agate, amethyst, bloodstone, carnelian, hematite, labradorite, black obsidian, quartz, smoky quartz, sunstone, tiger's eye, tourmaline

Petition words (or add your own sigil): Protection for me/ my family

Chant: *Dragon power bring to me*
          Strong protection I can feel and see
          Dragon roar, power within
          A circle of protection now bring in

Dragons in Ritual

Working a ritual to include dragons is a very powerful experience. You can call upon them to bring their elemental energy to the quarters and/or to work with you for the entire ritual. Just to reiterate, do not summon them, be polite and ask and, of course, they do love a bit of grandeur and flourish to your ritual requests.

Casting a circle using dragon energy works really well but you will need your visualisation skills. Whenever you are working a ritual, a spell or any kind of magic you need to 'feel' the energy, really feel it in your heart and soul. Just reading out the words is not going to cut it. Working a ritual or spell is all about raising and manipulating energy, if you do not do that then the whole thing is just pointless words (rant over). I like to start in the north direction when I cast a circle, walking clockwise. If you are short of space, you can turn around on the spot. See in your mind's eye the image of a large, long serpentine dragon and as you walk the circle see it slowly curling its body around to form a large circle. Call upon the dragon to create the circle for you:

Circle casting with dragon might
Keep us safe and within your sight
Protection now, within and without
Dragon magic circle is cast about

Dragon energy provides strong magic when they are invited into the quarters. You can place element candles at each main compass point or representations such as painted pebbles or dishes of corresponding herbs. Make sure you invite the dragons in, rather than demanding their presence. I start with north and work clockwise, lighting a candle in turn at each point. Most importantly you will need your visualisation skills for this, in fact for any ritual. As you invite each element in, open your third eye and 'see' a dragon forming at that compass point. Feel the energy of the dragon and visualise the qualities of each element. I associate North with earth, East with air, South with fire and Water with west, but you may have different associations.

Earth dragon energy, mighty and strong
Honour me with your magic in this ritual belong
Stability, grounding and strength beyond
Welcome oh mighty one

Air dragon energy, swift and strong
Honour me with your magic in this ritual belong
Intellect, intuition and insight beyond
Welcome oh mighty one

Fire dragon energy, passionate and strong
Honour me with your magic in this ritual belong
Power, energy and passion beyond
Welcome oh mighty one

Water dragon energy, fluid and strong

Honour me with your magic in this ritual belong
Emotions, psychic abilities and dreams beyond
Welcome oh mighty one

Once you have cast your circle and invited the dragons in from the four directions you are ready to work whatever magic your ritual is for. It might be a meditation to connect with dragons, it could be a spell or honouring a particular moon phase or sabbat. Dragon energy can be directed into any of these.

Once your magic is worked you will need to close down the ritual. Start by thanking the quarters. I do not use the term 'dismiss' because apart from sounding really bossy and rude, you can't dismiss dragon energy if it doesn't want to leave! On some level the dragons are always around us anyway so it would be quite pointless to try and remove them. It is better to just thank them for lending their energy to the ritual. Here are my suggested chants, thank the quarters in reverse order.

Water dragon energy, fluid and strong
Thank you for lending your energy to this ritual, I am honoured and blessed

Fire dragon energy, passionate and strong
Thank you for lending your energy to this ritual, I am honoured and blessed

Air dragon energy, swift and strong
Thank you for lending your energy to this ritual, I am honoured and blessed

Earth dragon energy, mighty and strong
Thank you for lending your energy to this ritual, I am honoured and blessed

As you thank each quarter visualise the energies dispersing, but do not force them if they want to stay.

Now you need to uncast your circle, I do this by walking anti clockwise around the circle and visualising the dragon uncurling and stretching out, sometimes he stays, other times he takes flight.

My circle was cast with dragon might
You kept me safe and within your site
You protected me, within and without
My thanks to you, and blessings about

After any ritual or spell work, I like to give an offering. I leave food for the birds or feed for the plants and trees. If I have had food or drink during the ritual, I place a little on the ground. For spell working in particular I give an offering of food or milk on my dragon altar.

Dragon Magic Ritual

The following is a ritual written by my coven, Kitchen Witch.[46] The intention was to run it as an open ritual outside in a beautiful forest setting. We had run rituals regularly in the same place for several years before. The ritual was discussed, planned, written and a date was set. Then bad weather hit and we had to postpone the ritual. A new date was set, then a pandemic hit with the associated lockdown so the ritual was put on hold indefinitely. Three years later we still haven't gotten around to holding the ritual, with the feeling that we were not supposed to. I suspect it was a lesson learnt to not include a chaos dragon. However, I have included the ritual script here, you might like to work it yourself, whether you choose to include the chaos dragon part I will leave up to you!

With my thanks to Ness, Josh, Heather, Sue and Gwyn for co-writing the ritual.

We divided the circle into four elements with chaos in the centre. At each point we placed a bowl of herbs that correspond with the element.

You will need:

A bowl for each of the four directions
Poppy seeds for air
Rice for earth
Rose petals for water
Bay leaves for fire
Chilli seeds for chaos
A small fabric pouch

Cast the circle, walking clockwise around.

With the power of ancient dragon magic
Cast the circle, with elements of four
Earth, air, fire, water
May the energy of all bring power and protection
This dragon magic circle is cast

Calling the quarters, facing each direction in turn.

East – Air Dragon
Air dragon, we humbly ask you to join us for our ritual today. Share with us your intellect, the realm of thought. Guide us with your clear, pure visualisation and your prowess of movement. Be the force that sends our visualisations out to become reality. Bring

us your energies to heal and shift our thoughts towards happiness, grace and acceptance.
We welcome you.

South – Fire Dragon

Fire dragon from the south, we call upon you to be with us here today during our ritual. We ask for your protection and help, to shield us from negative thoughts and energies. Please share with us your qualities of wisdom, passion, transformation, unity and balance of mind, body and spirit. Give us the courage to look inward, to find our own inner fire and to re-emerge like a butterfly from its chrysalis or the phoenix from the ashes, ready to move forward with a new found passion for life. The positive master of our own destinies.
We welcome you.

West – Water Dragon

We call to the water dragon in the west, mighty wyvern, we welcome you to our ritual. Share with us your gifts of healing and intuition, cleanse us of all negativity and fill us with peace, balance and positive energy. Guide us to be more loving and compassionate. Noble water dragon, you honour us with your presence.
We welcome you.

North – Earth Dragon

Earth dragon, we respectfully call upon your presence to our ritual. To wake from your deep earthly slumber and show us the power and potential that lies within us all. Nurture our bodies and minds. Help us ground our energies.
We welcome you.

Chaos Dragon

We call upon the chaos dragon, primordial energy of space and time. Embodiment of life, force of change. Catalyst of all that

has been and all there is to come. Help us to connect with the cosmic energy of the universe, to look within and find our divine selves. Compel us to surrender logic, to close our eyes to our own expectations so we may hear the whispering of silent truth.
We welcome you.

We are going to work with a dragon meditation. Be guided by your intuition and follow where it leads you. Once we have finished hopefully you will have connected with a dragon from a specific element. Begin by closing your eyes. Focus your attention on your breathing, in through the nose and out through the mouth.

As you become ever more relaxed, the world will begin to dissipate from around you, sending you to the middle of an immense plateau. Long shadows are cast across the rocky plains before you as the setting sun breaks through a cloud behind.

You look to your right to find the plains stretch out as far as you can see; huge mounds of rock, jaded and menacing, face the sky in all directions.

The clouds blanketing above you, streaked with magenta and violet, breaking in places to reveal the blues and purples behind them, the occasional twinkle of a lone star can be seen.

Your eyes are drawn to your left, the magnificent shimmering of a vast lake; the water, aglow from the setting sun, still and tranquil. So huge, you can barely make out the faint silhouettes of the forest trees on the opposite shore. But then, in the distance ahead of you, a flash of glorious colour catches your eye. What could have been a nondescript ashen mountain, is now dressed in wide rivers of deep crimson lava.

A dramatic geyser of flame erupts from the very top, followed closely by the largest bird you have ever seen. On second glance you release it to be a dragon. As you watch it dive in and out of the crater, peppering the land with more flecks of lava you spot another accompanying the first, plunging itself down towards the summit.

And then all at once, you notice that these two fire dragons are most definitely not alone.

On your right where you saw nothing but a boundless expanse, littered with an array of stone and boulder you know recognise the glint of a dozen earth dragon underbellies being sunned before dusk. Above you, you witness the air dragons. Weaves and lunges, somersaults and pirouettes, so fast you can barely follow, whipping and reshaping the clouds around them.

On your left the sunset bounces off the still water. Behind the near blinding shimmer of light, you discover beneath the surface, the gigantic forms of water dragons. Circling the depths of the lake, round and round, you hypnotically watch the school of dragons as they lap and twist with perfect synchronicity.

Take a moment to focus on the energy of this place, to reach out with your mind and connect with the power of the dragons around you. Find the dragon to whom you resonate the most, call them to you and ask if they would like to join you where you stand.

As the dragon lands before you, take the time to appreciate the connection you feel with them.

Notice their beauty, their aura, how they make you feel.

Take note of any sight, sound or smell that resonates or feels significant.

If you have any questions for them, receive permission before you ask them.

Should they wish to tell you something, listen carefully with an open heart and mind.

When you have finished with them, or they with you, bid them farewell.

Thank them for their presence, their guidance and their wisdom, knowing you may always return here to them, if ever you should need.

When you are ready, return your attention to your breathing once more.

Let your focus slowly shift from the land within your mind to the land beneath your feet.

Concentrate on the connection with Mother Earth beneath you.

When you feel comfortable open your eyes and come back to the here and now.

For each dragon you connect with, take a pinch of herbs from that element direction and add them to your pouch. Sit or stand in that element direction for a while and connect with those element sections. If you want to boost your dragon magic and bring about change, please do visit the centre of the circle and add a pinch of chaos dragon herbs to your pouch.

Air Dragons by Heather Dewhurst

Folk stories of air dragons being sighted have been told throughout all regions of the United Kingdom. Some believe the sightings were nothing more than the bright heads and dark forked tails of comments passing close to the earth. With enough imagination these comets might look like a flying dragon breathing fire. Others think the tales of dragons may have arisen from those wanting to keep the locals away from their stolen and hidden treasures. Whilst some stories may have even been created when exotic lizards from foreign regions escaped their owner and were seen in the wild.

Fire Dragons by Gwyneth Sangster

The key to dragon energy is balance and the fire dragon represents kingship, leadership and mastery. Its colour is read and it subsequently became the emblem for Wales and is still seen on the Welsh national flag. In mythology the fire dragon is often viewed as somewhat malignant but not to the Druids. They believed it to be neutral or having a 'mirror effect' being either malignant or benign based on how ready we are to take on the inner fire of our being. It reminds us that not all power is for everyone. The fire dragon only becomes malignant when we take on too much. As with everything, balance is a must both physically and psychologically. Abusing your inner fire dragon and its power can only create a fierce and fiery dangerous situation. Learning to befriend a fire dragon can promote vitality, enthusiasm and courage that can help you overcome obstacles in life. It can help us to learn where our limitations are and how to work around them. Once we learn how to balance stressful situations the fire dragon beings to fuel our inner fires allowing us to master leadership situations and to accomplish objectives.

Water Dragons by Sue Perryman

The water dragon brings connection, depth and passion. The water dragon as a power animal brings memories and wishes, perhaps long forgotten yet hidden, to the fore. By squaring up with painful past experiences, a sense of peace and balance can be achieved in our lives. The water dragon will give you courage and compassion in this challenge.

Earth Dragons by Ness Armstrong

These dragons are ruled by Grael (pronounced grail), their elemental colour is pure green, and their homes are in cold and dry places. Earth dragons are very quiet beings, they will observe from a distance until they are ready to approach you. Once you have befriended an earth dragon they are very straight forward and will be blunt and honest with you but can be loving and nurturing. Of all the dragons these are the ones that like treasure and in order to build a strong relationship you should keep a jar or dish full of coins.

Chaos Dragon by Joshua Petchey

The largest of their kind, long and serpentine in form, chaos dragons are always the darkest of colours. Most commonly portrayed in purple, chaos dragons actually don many colours of the rainbow, but always in a shade almost black. These beautiful creatures throughout history have often been mislabelled as evil or malicious. This is, of course, untrue. Chaos in itself is a primordial energy. It exists in everything and everyone and is the creative force of the universe. It is often misunderstood and brings about images of great destruction and the world in disarray. But this is only because we fear the unknown and the unpredictability of chaos. Sometimes in life problems cannot be solved with order and reasoning and the chaos dragon is then called. They are called often for big changes in one's life. The recreation of careers and love lives, the reversal of spells gone awry, the reversal of life decisions that were disastrous. It will find the very source of the problem and turn you to the correct path to solve it. But it is often warned not to call on the chaos dragon for aid with your issues if you are not willing to accept the solution.

Drumming followed by feasting. We recommend ginger cake and ginger beer or ginger tea.

Release the quarters:

Chaos Dragon, unencumbered by the chains of time, you have opened our eyes to this hidden knowledge. Shown us the way past reason and emotion to reveal the divine self within.

May we go forth resonating with the primordial energy that is the very foundation of our universe.

We thank you.

Earth dragon, you may return to your deep earthly slumber. You have shown us the potential to be powerful in mind and spirit. We feel nurtured and grounded. We thank you for your presence in our ritual today.

Water dragon, return to your crystal-clear waters if you will. We thank you for joining us in our ritual, for sharing with us your gifts and wisdom and for guiding us through the ebb and flow of life.

Dragon of fire, may we continue to move forward in life with increasing passion and the ability to master whatever obstacles life may put in our way. As you return to the fiery lands of the south, we thank you for joining us today.

Air Dragon, thank you for joining us here today. As you take flight from here, continue your watch over our thoughts and wishes, to bring us happiness, acceptance and serenity. We thank you for joining us today.

Close the circle:

With the power of ancient dragon magic and the elements of four
Earth, air, fire, water
May the energy of all carry with us
This circle is open but never broken

Dragon Grounding

After any kind of energy work it is advisable to ground, it helps release any excess energy you have remaining. Not grounding can leave you feeling light headed or even give you a head ache. There are lots of different methods for grounding, visualising yourself as a tree is the most usual one, sending your roots down into the earth and releasing excess energy. You can just stamp your feet or clap your hands and placing your palms on the earth to release the energy works well too.

If you have worked a dragon ritual you can release excess energy into the dragon that formed the circle. Ask permission first and then place your hands onto the dragon and release any excess energy. The dragon will usually be very willing to do this.

For grounding at any other time, you can visualise a dragon before you, if you have a guardian dragon then it works very well. Otherwise ask that a dragon come to you to accept any excess energy. Once you see the dragon you can place your hands on it and give your energy. You do not necessarily need to physically see the dragon, sometimes you may just feel it nearby, ask if you can release your excess energy and ground using its power and it will hopefully oblige.

Dragon Protection

If you want to conquer the world, you best have dragons.
George R. R. Martin

Some of you may be familiar with shielding, the use of visualisation to create a psychic protective, flexible bubble around you to keep out unwanted negative energy. Particularly useful in any situation where there are crowds of people or when you feel overwhelmed by the emotions or energy of others. Whilst the bubble shield is a classic method and very useful, once you have a guardian dragon they can help you with this. If you feel the need to shield, ask your dragon to step up and protect you. You probably won't see it, but you will feel a cloak of energy being drawn around you.

I have also on occasion requested assistance from my fire dragon to protect my home, he usually obliges without too much complaint. Having an enormous fire breathing dragon sitting on the roof of your home protecting it whilst you are away is very beneficial.

Cleansing

It is surprising how quickly negative energy can build up in your home, it can be brought in unknowingly from outside by family and friends or even carried in on physical items. We are probably all also guilty of creating our own negative energy at times too. The usual method to clear negative energy within a house is to smudge with smoke and it works very well. You can help by bringing in dragon energy to really clear away the unwanted vibes. This can be done by smoke alone, using a cleansing dragon energy incense (recipe below). Alternatively, you can ask for dragon breath assistance. Nothing clears out stale or stagnant energy than a good blast with dragon breath. That is not to say you have the right to use your dragon as a smudge stick, you will still need to be polite and ask and a repayment of an offering helps too. Ask your dragon if it is willing to help and then walk around your home, visualising your dragon walking with you, breathing dragon breath into all the corners and watching it eat up any negative energy. Do not forget to thank your dragon for its help.

Your dragon can also help clear any negative energy that has become attached to your body. Sit quietly and call upon your dragon and ask it to scan you to see if you have any negative energy that needs clearing. Your dragon will usually oblige and may even give you some suggestions for bringing in protection in the future. It will then hopefully clear the negative vibes away for you as well, be prepared because this usually comes in the form of a blast of dragon breath or even flames.

Cleansing Dragon Incense

2 parts dragon's blood resin
2 parts mugwort
1 part sandalwood
A few drops of mint essential oil

Musical Dragons

Dragons love vibrations of all kinds particularly within the realms of music and dance. I like to work with my drum and the dragons seem to respond to the beat very well. But do not be limited by just a drum beat. Try different types of beats from drums, rattles, cymbals and bells. You may also find that your dragon loves a bit of heavy metal, 80s pop or opera, they have a wide range of musical tastes.

Sabbat and Seasonal Dragons

Noble dragons don't have friends. The nearest they can get to the idea is an enemy who is still alive. Terry Pratchett

An interesting way to work with dragons is in a seasonal capacity. Linking to a different dragon for each season or sabbat. This can help you gain a greater understanding of dragons and how they work in tune with nature. Dragons do not really work with the world on a linear basis because they are so in tune with nature and her movements, they do seem to recognise the changing of the seasons and the flow of energy that comes with the sabbats.

Call upon a dragon for each sabbat or season to join you in your magical workings, in ritual or just to walk you through working with the energy of each time frame. You may find you are met by one dragon to take you through the whole year or four dragons, one to work with you for each season. You may even discover eight different dragons, each one aligning with the sabbats. Ask for them to join you in meditation or just by putting out a request and be open to whoever turns up.

I am sure you are familiar with the dates of the sabbats, but here they are with some ideas of magic that can be worked in harmony and partnership with dragons. I tend to work with the sabbats over a span of a few weeks rather than just the one date, the energy ebbs and flows like the phases of the moon. Energy building up in the weeks before the date of the sabbat and waning for a few weeks afterwards. Remember Mother Nature does not read dates on a calendar, neither do dragons so keep a connection with the weather and seasonal patterns in your area. The dates given here reflect the traditional dates in both the northern and southern hemispheres.

Imbolc - 2ⁿᵈ February/1ˢᵗ August

Bringing the very first shy signs of spring, but most of the awakening is done beneath the soil. This is a time to work magic for plotting, planning and scheming getting new ideas ready.

Spring Equinox/Ostara - 20–23 March/20-23 September

The Spring Equinox brings fertility in all forms full of new growth and fresh beginnings. It is also a time of balance when day and night are of equal length.

Beltane - 1ˢᵗ May/31ˢᵗ October

A festival full to bursting with passionate, creative fire energy, Beltane rocks into place packed full of fertility and growth magic.

Summer Solstice/Litha - 20-22 June/21–22 December

A celebration of the longest day and shortest night, the summer solstice is full of solar magic. Nature is in full growing season and the sun is shining bringing with it the magic of happiness and luck.

Lughnasadh (sometimes called Lammas) - 1ˢᵗ August/2ⁿᵈ February

The first of the harvest celebrations is Lughnasadh, a time to be thankful for all that Mother Nature provides. The energy of this sabbat is about harvesting what we have sown for ourselves and adding in some gratitude too.

Autumn Equinox/Mabon - 20–23 September/20–23 March

The autumn equinox is the second harvest celebration of the year and also welcomes the balance of the equinox. The energy is all about clearing out, refreshing and balance.

Samhain - 31ˢᵗ October/1ˢᵗ May

The end of summer is marked by the festival of Samhain. This is the time of year to remember those that have gone before us and to make preparations for the dark months ahead.

Winter Solstice/Yule - 21–22 December/20–22 June

The time of year to spend with family and friends, to celebrate and ride the wave of festive energy. We honour the shortest day and longest night to welcome back the sun.

If you prefer to work with the four seasons rather than the sabbats, the dragons will usually be happy to do that too.

- Spring is all about new growth, life and renewal and for me it heralds the real start of each year. Spring relates to the element of air and brings the magic of new beginnings, planning, planting seeds, creativity and potential.
- Summer brings the sun, hopefully anyway and Mother Nature is literally in full swing. Summer relates to the element of fire and brings the magic of growth, abundance, happiness, power and protection.
- Autumn is a time of change, when summer fades and the trees take on their beautiful autumn hues. Autumn relates to the element of water and brings the magic of transitions, harvest, knowledge, travel and success.
- Winter gives us a chance to rest and recuperate, a time for hibernation to work on inner magic. Winter relates to the element of earth and brings the magic of releasing, transformation, guidance, truth and inner work.

Dragon Crystals

For those that like to work with crystals there are a few that align themselves very nicely with dragon energy. If you can get hold of a dragon skull shaped crystal then even better.

Cinnabar

Cinnabar or cinnabarite is a mercury sulphide mineral. Be careful is this does make the stone toxic, remember to wash your hands after handling. Cinnabar was formed by ancient volcanic activity that occurred near to natural hot springs. The name cinnabar translates to 'dragon's blood'. This is a stone of transformation, truth, manifestation and self-discovery.

Dragon's Blood Jasper

Quite an unusual one which might be difficult to find, dragon's blood jasper is a blend of green fuchsite and red jasper, usually only found in Western Australia. This stone is full of bravery and courage that also helps solve any problems or issues. Folk tales suggest this stone is the petrified remains of ancient dragons, the green being dragon skin and the red the blood of the dragon.

Dragon Blood Jasper/Dragon Stone/Dragon Bloodstone

Often confused with the Australian dragon's blood jasper, this one is a mixture of epidote and piedmontite minerals which puts it in the chalcedony family rather than a true jasper. This one brings the energy of kundalini, the dragon energy. It can help with big life changes, reaching your goals and bringing creativity and courage.

Dragon Egg

Dragon egg crystals are usually a natural clear quartz in a rough egg shape with one side polished clear. Clear quartz is an excellent 'all-rounder' crystal to work with. Clear quartz is a master healer and can be used to amplify the power of other crystals.

Septarian

Often called the Dragon Stone, septarian is a tri colour crystal composed of aragonite, calcite and limestone. Septarian is a strong earth energy stone that can help with grounding and connection to nature. It also helps with changes and inner awakenings. Septarian is a powerful protection stone that can help strengthen your aura. This stone works well for past life work and journeying, full of ancient wisdom and ancestor magic.

Dragon Herbs, Plants and Foods

As I love working with magical herbs, I will often create an incense blend or spell pouch to help me connect and work with dragon energy. Some plants and herbs lend themselves to dragon energy very nicely, here are my suggestions.

Bistort (Bistort P. bistorta)

Ancient texts and stories often use the folk name for plants and particularly appear in tales where witches are throwing eye of newt and wing of bag into a large bubbling cauldron. These are just folk names and not the actual animal body part. One of these is 'dragon's scales' which is the leaf from the bistort plant. Bistort is also known as snake weed, serpentaria, dracunculus, serpentary dragonwort and oderwort. Bistort brings a strong protective energy along with luck and prosperity.

Delphinium/Larkspur

Delphinium flowers (sometimes called larkspur) is a huge genus of plants ranging from tiny alpine flowers to shrubs. Note, this plant is poisonous if ingested. Tales tell of delphinium flowers being created from drops of dragon blood falling upon the ground, so it has a good connection with dragon magic. Delphinium brings the magic of protection and a strong fairy world connection.

Dragon's Blood

An obvious choice, of course. Dragon's blood is usually found in resin form and comes from the Daemonorops genus of trees, but also from the Dracaena species. Ancient lore states that dragon's blood resin is the dried blood from dragons that died in mortal combat. It carried the power of dragon magic and works well for adding power to spells, protection, love and happiness.

Dragon Fruit

The dragon fruit looks amazing, such a beautiful and weird fruit, the outer skin looks like...yep, you guessed it, dragon skin. The dragon fruit is a pitaya, a fruit from several different cactus species. The bright pinky-red outer skin has soft green spikes and the inside is a white flesh speckled with tiny black seeds. Peel the skin and dry it to use in magical workings and eat the inside because it is delicious. The peel will not add any scent to incense blends, but it will bring the power of dragon energy in the form of courage, strength, bravery and warrior vibes to any spell working. Dragon fruit also works well in any workings to bring about protection. Legend tells the dragon fruit was created during a battle between and Emperor and his soldiers against a fire breathing dragon. When the dragon spewed fire it left behind these fruits. Those that ate the fruit were filled with strength and bravery. The dragon fruit is also believed to bring about good luck and fortune along with transformation and new beginnings.

Dragon's Tongue

The Hemigraphis repanda is often called the Dragon's Tongue plant. A tropical grass like plant, it has dark green/purple foliage and the leaves have rippled edges along with small white or pink flowers. Use the fresh or dried leaves or flowers in magical workings to bring on the dragon energy particularly anything fire element related or to do with communication.

Dragon's tail

The epipremnum pinnatum plant carries the name Dragon's Tail plant and is generally used as a house plant originating in tropical rainforests. Obviously, it can be used for all kinds of dragon magic but as it has a rainforest connection and loves lots of water it works well for water element magic. With the dragon tail connection, it also brings in a huge punch of protection magic.

Milk

A huge amount of folk tales and myths tell that dragon's love to drink milk. Milk has a strong feminine energy and an association with the moon, it brings a wonderful nurturing magic.

Pine

Evergreen conifer trees, the needles and bark work very well in all kinds of dragon magic, they also bring protection, focus, truth, abundance, fertility, healing and purification.

Pine nut

The seeds from the Pinaceae family also carry the same energies as the pine needles. These can be eaten to imbue dragon magic or added to spell workings.

Snapdragon

The antirrhinum majus carries the folk name of snapdragon, the flowers resembling the head and mouth of a dragon. Folk lore suggests that antirrhinums were placed on the graves of successful dragon slayers. The snapdragon has a strong elemental energy so it is perfect for all kinds of dragon magic along with protection, truth, divination and keeping nightmares away.

Tarragon

Also known as dragon's mugwort, wyrmwort or little dragon. The roots of the plant grow twisty and intertwine with each other, like snakes. The Latin name for tarragon is 'artemisia dracunculus' which translates as 'little dragon'. It is believed the herb could cure the bit of a dragon. The roots of the plant also curl around, making them look like a dragon's tail. Tarragon brings courage, confidence, protection and a boost for helping you grow.

Dragon's Blood Ink

When writing magical petitions or prayers to dragons you could use dragon's blood ink. The dragon will not be offended as it doesn't use real blood. Grind dragon's blood resin to a fine powder and add a little water, stir until the powder dissolves and add extra water a little at a time until you get a liquid that can be used as ink.

Dragon Breathing

Within the practise of yoga there is a form of breathing called dragon breath. This is a wonderful exercise to help calm you down if you find yourself in a stressful or emotional situation. It focuses on drawing in deep slow breaths that help slow down your breathing, heart rate and blood pressure. This sends signals to our brain that the stressful situation has passed and we need to calm down. I would recommend learning this practice when you are already feeling calm, work with it and then when you need to use it in an emergency you are already well versed with how it works.

- Breathing normally, place one hand on your belly and feel your stomach move in and out when you breathe.
- Take a long slow deep breath in through your nose and fill your lungs as much as you can, feel how your stomach moves.
- Now let go of your breath sending it out through your open mouth just as a dragon would breathe fire. Feel how your stomach moves on the outward breath.

- Repeat the exercise, long slow breathes in to fill your lungs as much as you can then long whooshes of breath out through your mouth.

You are dragon breathing!

A Dragon's Tail

And so, to the tail ending of this introduction to dragon's and their magic. This journey will be one of amazing discovery, if you are prepared to put the work in. I wholeheartedly encourage you to give it your all, you will not be disappointed.

I believe in fairies, the myths, dragons. It all exists, even if it's in your mind. Who's to say that dreams and nightmares aren't as real as the here and now? — John Lennon

Endnotes

1. https://www.etymonline.com/
2. https://www.oxfordlearnersdictionaries.com/
3. Robert Plot - Natural History of Oxfordshire, first published in 1677
4. https://www.atlasobscura.com/
5. Albert Koch's Hydrarchos Craze, Lukas Rieppel
6. https://www.newworldencyclopedia.org/entry/Apollonius_of_Tyana
7. https://www.theoi.com/Thaumasios/OphiesPteretoi.html
8. The Rig Veda: Complete (Illustrated) 18 Feb. 2017 by Anonymous (Author), Ralph T. H. Griffith (Translator)
9. https://www.worldhistory.org/article/225/enuma-elish---the-babylonian-epic-of-creation---fu/
10. https://www.britannica.com/topic/Apopis-Egyptian-god
11. Revelation 12:9
12. https://www.theoi.com/greek-mythology/dragons.html
13. Of Dragons, Basilisks and the Arms of the Seven Kings of Rome, Helmut Nickel, 1989
14. https://norse-mythology.org/gods-and-creatures/giants/jormungand/
15. Dragonships, Tekst Marit Synnove Vea, https://avaldsnes.info/
16. The Song of Canute, Saga of St. Olaf)
17. https://www.mysteriousbritain.co.uk/ancient-sites/cadbury-castle/
18. https://folklorescotland.com/assipattle-and-the-mester-stoor-worm/
19. The History and Antiquities of the County Palatine of Durham, Surtees, Robert (1820)
20. The Mordiford Dragon, Devlin Dacres. J (1848)

21. https://www.mysteriousbritain.co.uk/legends/dragon-of-aller/
22. https://www.constellation-guide.com/constellation-list/draco-constellation/
23. The Hobbit, J. R. R. Tolkien
24. The Jabberwocky, C S Lewis
25. Harry Potter and the Goblet of Fire, J K Rowling
26. Chris d'Lacey, Fire World
27. Guards! Guards", Terry Pratchett
28. Pamphlet published in 1875, Newcastle-upon-Tyne by T Arthur and A Everatt
29. The Rig Veda (Penguin Classics) by Wendy Doniger
30. https://www.originalbuddhas.com/about-buddha-statues/naga-buddha-statues-with-snake
31. https://www.chinabeastsandlegends.com/ying-long
32. https://www.worldhistory.org/Ryujin/
33. Enuma Elish, Babylonian creation myth - https://www.worldhistory.org/article/225/enuma-elish
34. https://allaboutdragons.com/dragons/Zilant
35. Homeric Hymn Three, Metamorphoses (Ovid), Euripides, Theogony (Hesiod)
36. Euthydemus (Plato), Pseudo-Apollodorus, Bibliotheca, Diodorus Siculus, Library of History, Quintus Smyrnaeus, Fall of Troy
37. Revelations 12:7–9
38. Revelations 12: 13–17
39. Revelations 20: 1-3, 7–10)
40. Legenda aurea/Golden Legend, Jacob de Voragine (1265) - https://www.britannica.com/biography/Saint-George
41. The Poetic Edda, The Saga of Volsungs, Jesse Byock (1990)
42. History of the Kings of Britain, Geoffrey of Monmouth (c 1136)
43. https://www.bl.uk/medieval-english-french-manuscripts/articles/beastly-tales-from-the-medieval-bestiary

44. Tanakh is the Hebrew Bible, the collection of Jewish texts, which is also the source for most of the Christian Old Testament

45. https://brendan-noble.com/zmij-zmey-dragons-of-slavic-mythology-slavic-saturday/

46. www.kitchenwitchhearth.net

Recommended Further Reading

Arnold, Martin – The Dragon Fear and Power (2018)

Bruce, Scott – The Penguin Book of Dragons (2021)

Evans, Jonathan – Dragons Myth & Legend (2008)

Freeman, Richard – Dragons, more than a myth (2005)

Freeman, Richard – Explore Dragons (2006)

MacKenzie, Shawn – Dragons for Beginners (2012)

McCullough, Joseph A – Dragonslayers (2013)

Simpson, Jacqueline – British Dragons (2001)

www.cfz.org.uk (The Centre for Fortean Zoology)

About the Author

I am an English witch who has been walking the Pagan pathway for over thirty years. A working wife and mother who has been lucky enough to have had over 25 books published (so far), some of them becoming best sellers. My passion is to learn, I love to study and have done so from books, online resources, schools and wonderful mentors over the years and still continue to learn each and every day, but I have learnt the most from actually getting outside and doing it.

I like to laugh ... and eat cake...

It is my pleasure to give talks to pagan groups and co-run open rituals and workshops run by the Kitchen Witch Coven. I am also High Priestess of the Kitchen Witch Coven and an Elder at the online Kitchen Witch School of Natural Witchcraft.

A regular columnist with Fate & Fortune magazine, I also contribute articles to several magazines such as Pagan Dawn and Witchcraft & Wicca. You will find my regular ramblings on my own personal blog and YouTube channel.

My craft is a combination of old religion witchcraft, Wicca, hedge witchery, kitchen witchery and folk magic. My heart is that of an English Kitchen Witch.

It was my honour to be added to the Watkins 'Spiritual 100 List' for 2023.

www.rachelpatterson.co.uk
facebook.com/rachelpattersonbooks

www.kitchenwitchhearth.net
facebook.com/kitchenwitchuk
Email: HQ@kitchenwitchhearth.net

www.youtube.com/user/Kitchenwitchuk
www.instagram.com/racheltansypatterson

MY BOOKS

Kitchen Witchcraft Series
Spells & Charms
Garden Magic
Crystal Magic
The Element of Earth
The Element of Fire
The Element of Water

Pagan Portals
Kitchen Witchcraft
Hoodoo Folk Magic
Moon Magic
Meditation
The Cailleach
Animal Magic
Sun Magic
Triple Goddess
Gods & Goddesses of England

Other Moon Books
The Art of Ritual
Beneath the Moon
Witchcraft ... into the Wilds
Grimoire of a Kitchen Witch

A Kitchen Witch's World of Magical Foods
A Kitchen Witch's World of Magical Plants & Herbs
Arc of the Goddess (co-written with Tracey Roberts)
Moon Books Gods & Goddesses Colouring Book
(Patterson family)
Practically Pagan: An Alternative Guide to Cooking

Llewellyn
Curative Magic
A Witch for Every Season
Practical Candle Magic

Solarus
Flower Magic Oracle Deck

Animal Dreaming Publishing
Kitchen Witchcraft Oracle Deck Series

MOON BOOKS
PAGANISM & SHAMANISM

What is Paganism? A religion, a spirituality, an alternative belief system, nature worship? You can find support for all these definitions (and many more) in dictionaries, encyclopaedias, and text books of religion, but subscribe to any one and the truth will evade you. Above all Paganism is a creative pursuit, an encounter with reality, an exploration of meaning and an expression of the soul. Druids, Heathens, Wiccans and others, all contribute their insights and literary riches to the Pagan tradition. Moon Books invites you to begin or to deepen your own encounter, right here, right now.

If you have enjoyed this book, why not tell other readers by posting a review on your preferred book site.

Bestsellers from Moon Books

Keeping Her Keys
An Introduction to Hekate's Modern Witchcraft
Cyndi Brannen
*Blending Hekate, witchcraft and personal development together
to create a powerful new magickal perspective.*
Paperback: 978-1-78904-075-3 ebook 978-1-78904-076-0

Journey to the Dark Goddess
How to Return to Your Soul
Jane Meredith
*Discover the powerful secrets of the Dark Goddess and transform
your depression, grief and pain into healing and integration.*
Paperback: 978-1-84694-677-6 ebook: 978-1-78099-223-5

Shamanic Reiki
Expanded Ways of Working with Universal Life Force Energy
Llyn Roberts, Robert Levy
*Shamanism and Reiki are each powerful ways of healing; together,
their power multiplies. Shamanic Reiki introduces techniques to
help healers and Reiki practitioners tap ancient healing wisdom.*
Paperback: 978-1-84694-037-8 ebook: 978-1-84694-650-9

Southern Cunning
Folkloric Witchcraft in the American South
Aaron Oberon
*Modern witchcraft with a Southern flair, this book is a journey
through the folklore of the American South and a look at the power
these stories hold for modern witches.*
Paperback: 978-1-78904-196-5 ebook: 978-1-78904-197-2

For video content, author interviews and more, please subscribe to our YouTube channel.

MoonBooksPublishing

Follow us on social media for book news, promotions and more:

Facebook: Moon Books

Instagram: @MoonBooksCI

Twitter: @MoonBooksCI

TikTok: @MoonBooksCI